# *Discover Bob Grant's savvy, forthright thinking on what's right and what's wrong with America:*

**TAXES:** The flat tax, in my opinion, is the only way to fix things. . . . It would allow us to disband the IRS, which is secretive, evil, and incompetent.

**POLITICAL CORRECTNESS:** This republic was founded to escape the brutality of King George, who would brook no disagreement. And now we're right back to that—living among tyrants who allow no alternative viewpoint. People can no longer express a true sentiment if it runs counter to the world view of the P.C. Police.

**ANIMAL RIGHTS ACTIVISTS:** The big cry in the animal rights movement is this: "A rat is a pig is a dog is a boy." In other words, a rat has the same rights as a person. Touching. But why stop there? Why isn't a cabbage a rat? Why isn't seaweed? Algae? Moss? They're all living things, too. What about equal rights for bacteria?

**BILINGUAL EDUCATION:** The multiculturalists . . . [will] be happy when this country resembles a Tower of Babel with no central culture, no backbone holding us all together.

# BOB GRANT

## LET'S BE HEARD

**POCKET BOOKS**

New York   London   Toronto   Sydney   Tokyo   Singapore

POCKET BOOKS, a division of Simon & Schuster Inc.
1230 Avenue of the Americas, New York, NY 10020

Grant, Bob.
    Let's be heard. The king of conservative talk radio speaks out to America / Bob Grant.
        p.   cm.
    ISBN: 0-671-53721-0
    1. United States—Politics and government—1993–   2. United States—Social conditions—1980–   3. Talk shows—United States   4. Radio journalism—United States.   I. Title.
E885.G72   1996
973.929—dc20                                                                 95-53163
                                                                                CIP

First Pocket Books trade paperback printing March 1997

10   9   8   7   6   5   4   3   2   1

Cover design by Joseph Perez
Cover photo by Robert Clark

Printed in the U.S.A.

*This book is dedicated to all the people who urged me to write it.*

# *Acknowledgments*

I want to start by acknowledging some people who operate behind the scenes of my show. Even listeners probably don't know their names, but to me they are vitally important. I'm speaking here about my strong, loyal, and supportive bosses, three men who have always stood by me when the going got tough. Don Boloukos is a good friend as well as a dependable leader, Mike Mallardi has gracefully withstood the heat and hate mail that my program visits upon ABC's top brass, and Jim Arcara is a true visionary in the radio business. Without them, there would be no real freedom of expression on my show, and so I thank them with my head and heart.

I also wish to thank the following good people, for without their efforts, abilities, and assistance, this book would not exist: Emily Bestler, George Hiltzik, John Mainelli, Richard Pine, Josephine Saracco, and Bill Tonelli. They have my eternal gratitude.

# Contents

◆

# Contents

# Contents

# *Before You Buy This Book . . .*

. . . ASSUMING, OF COURSE, THAT THE MERE PRESENCE OF MY NAME and handsome visage on the cover weren't enough to instantly send you to the cashier with several copies in hand . . .

Before you buy this book, consider this:

There are plenty of highly educated, hard-working experts, people of goodwill and energy, who are far more qualified than I to prescribe remedies for improving the quality of life in this country.

**They're the reason we're in such a horrible mess.**

There are also many dedicated, noble statesmen and public servants who have devoted their very lives to guiding America to a brighter future.

**They've screwed it up unbelievably, even worse than any of us knows.**

Then, of course, there are the acres of activists, pundits, philosophers, and other freelance geniuses who hold millions spellbound with their wisdom on what's wrong with our nation.

**Geez, don't even get me started on those fake, phony frauds.**

So, in the spirit of the Founding Fathers, who envisioned a nation that would be guided by determined private citizens of genuine concern and ideals—not career politicians, not self-serving bureaucrats, not special-interest hucksters who promote the minority at the expense of the majority—I am about to open my mouth and speak my mind.

I've been doing that for more than forty years on the radio in New York and Los Angeles. I've been at the barricades in every social and political battle you can name—from forced busing to affirmative action, from the commie menace to the multicultural wars. There's been one constant through all those hours on the air: I've always made people mad.

I can't help it. Name anybody you want; there's no other broadcaster alive who has inspired the sheer volume of anger, rage, apoplexy, hysteria, and brain-fevered, full-throated howls of indignation and injury that I have. As they say, the truth hurts, and so I consider every wound I've inflicted to be a badge of honor.

I may *already* have made you mad, and I haven't even gotten warmed up. But let's not allow *that* to get in the way of a good time. I hear a lot of weeping and moaning these days about "angry white men." It's funny—when everybody *but* white men was getting angry, it was considered to be a positive and healthy liberating expression of honest, righteous grievances. Once white males finally got angry, too, anger suddenly became a nasty, destructive force. But it's *fun* to get angry once in a while, especially when it seems so deserved. It keeps your blood flowing and your heart kicking. It brings a glow to your complexion. It feels so good.

Let's rock.

# LET'S BE HEARD

# My Low-Tech Lynching

———— ◆ ————

TODAY I'M A HERO.

I arrive at the studio where I do my show, high above Madison Square Garden, and find that I can't go five steps without being stopped and congratulated. Salespeople, secretaries, technicians, even my tough-to-impress manager—all of them are practically gleeful at the sight of me. At first I don't even know what I did to deserve all these hosannas. Then I hear that the new ratings book is out early, and my show has not only held on to its usual number-one spot, it has gotten an unprecedented 7.1 rating. Through the roof.

Let me tell you, in my business there can be no better news. If you think you're any good at this, you want to do it up big—more listeners, lots of stations, larger presence, greater influence. And here I am today, after more than forty years in the trade, bigger than ever.

What accounts for this new peak in my popularity? Am I suddenly smarter than before, more charming, newly irresistible? Don't make me laugh. My ratings zoomed as a result of the absolute, no-contest, certifiably worst crisis of my professional life: a time when I was vilified on the front pages of newspapers and magazines and demonized on the radio and TV airwaves. A time when I felt lower—more betrayed, ostracized, and scorned—than ever before. To be perfectly honest, before it was over, I was so disgusted that I damn near walked out on radio for good.

It all began rather happily six months earlier, when I got a call from a local rag, *New York* magazine, saying they wanted to do a feature on me, a cover story. Years ago, the same magazine sent a true-blue-liberal woman writer out to profile me, but the piece that ran was balanced and fair and accurate. They even titled it, "The Man You Hate to Love." So of course, I was glad to get this call, even though never for a second did I believe that I would be their cover boy. I've been doing the show in New York for twenty-five years by now, and there's not much new or newsworthy in that. So I thought.

Anyway, they sent a photographer up here to shoot me in the studio. It was at that session that I should have seen the sucker punch coming. During the course of the shoot, somobody from the magazine asked me to take one of the WABC banners that hang on the wall, wrap it around my shoulders, and strike a pose as though I were orating to the city of New York. I loved the idea, but only because I'm a ham. So I allowed the photographer's assistant to wrap the silly thing around me, and I stuck my index finger up in the air, and they took the picture.

Fine and dandy so far. Then the reporter came around to interview me. He presented himself very politely, properly, professionally. I had no problem with his approach at all. Now, I pride myself on giving an honest interview. My fiancée says I'm too honest. And she's probably right. But I answered the guy truthfully. He asked a great number of the usual questions, and then he finally got around to the hot one, the one I knew he had hidden in his back pocket all along, like a blackjack:

"Bob," he said, all but rubbing his hands together, "are you a racist?"

Ho-hum. *How predictable.* Believe me, there's no conservative in this country, white, black, or any other color, who hasn't had to answer that terrible accusation. It goes with the territory, and I'll explain why later. Unlike so many others I could name, I have never been spineless about voicing my views on the enormous, damaging role race plays in our society. So I said, "Well, look—I'm asked this question often. And there are a lot of ways I could answer it. I could answer it by saying, 'No more than *you* are.' " And that's a good way to answer, because when I say that, a person has to think to himself: *Uh, am I racist?* And let's face it—there isn't a soul alive who at one point or another doesn't have a racist thought. Blacks do, whites do, Asians do, everybody does.

But instead I said, "Well, if being *against* affirmative action and busing, if being for civil rights for *all* people—including whites—makes me a racist, then I plead guilty."

Again, having to answer a nasty, insulting question like that is nothing new for me, so the interview proceeded smoothly from there. The reporter called later with some follow-up questions, and again, he was very polite, and again, I was very cooperative.

And then we didn't hear a thing. I asked the station's publicist if she knew anything, and she said only that she'd heard the piece would be coming out soon. I asked if it was going to be the cover, and she said she still didn't know.

Well, "soon" came and went, and no story appeared. Finally I wrote it off as just another false alarm.

Then out of the blue, three months later, I got a call from an editor at the magazine telling me that they definitely were going to run the story next week. I asked, "Is it going to be a cover?" And she hesitated, then said in a mealy-mouthed voice, "Well, I'm not *sure* . . ." Which I now know was an out-and-out lie.

So it was a fine Saturday night in October when I first saw the fruits of the magazine's conscientious labors. I was doing a TV appearance that night and was eager to see an advance copy, but I didn't want to give them my home address, so I had the magazine messenger a copy to the Reo Diner, in Woodbridge, New Jersey, my home away from home.

I left my friends in the car outside, ran into the diner, and ripped open the waiting envelope.

And then—I went into shock.

I called my friends in and said I had something to show them.

They looked. *They* went into shock.

We were all dumbstruck as we gazed at the cover—a big picture of me accompanied by the headline: "WHY HE HATES BLACKS."

I was so repulsed by the thing, I shoved it back in the envelope. I couldn't even look at it. I barely slept that night.

First thing Sunday, I attempted some damage control. I called John Mainelli, WABC's then program director, and I said, "John, I understand that Lynn Samuels [a fellow host] is going to be plugging my appearance on the cover of *New York* magazine on her show today. Please, tell her *not* to say one thing!" John asked why not, and I said, "Believe me— it's *devastating*."

Still, operating on the principle that no publicity is bad publicity, John said nothing to Lynn, and she promoted the wretched thing. So I called John back, and I could tell he was thinking, *What's Grant so upset about?* I said, "John, have you *seen* the magazine?" And he admitted, "Well, we didn't get our copy yet." I said, "I guarantee you, once you see it, you'll understand why I'm making this request."

The fun started bright and early Monday morning, the day the magazine hit the stands. I tuned in the famed radio sleazeball Howard Stern, figuring he'd feast on my misfortune. Sure enough, Howard was talking and laughing about it, making racial comments far harsher and meaner than anything I was guilty of. His sidekick, Robin, was reading a news story about a woman who had been attacked, and in doing the story she said that the police identified the assailant as an African-American. And Howard laughed and said, "An African-American! I can't believe it!! Surprise, surprise!!! A black guy committed a crime? What do you know?" Then he got back to picking on me a little bit, but it was good-natured and funny.

When I got into the studio, an obviously upset John Mainelli told me that *New York* magazine had had the nerve to call him and ask if I would please go on local TV news to be interviewed about the piece. They actually wanted me to help them sell magazines! Without even consulting me, John told them in no uncertain terms what they could do with their interview. And then we made the decision that I wouldn't comment on the article at all and give it enough time—oh, a day or two—to blow over.

Pretty naive, right? I just figured that I wasn't quoted saying anything I hadn't been saying for years and years, on the radio, in print, and everywhere else. The article quoted me attacking my *paesano* Mario Cuomo and lots of other white liberal menaces to society. So, except for the libelous cover line, what was the big deal?

But I hadn't accounted for how the political climate around me had changed. Today, people—even mere radio announcers—who dare to express opinions that are strong and free and genuine are made to suffer. Once the Political Correctness Gang and the Special Interests Posse hear something they don't like, it's curtains, my friend.

The first call for my head went up a few days later. It was made by a bunch of black so-called ministers who have nothing better to do all day than shoot off their mouths for the TV cameras. They assembled on the steps of the New Jersey capitol, in Trenton, read a proclamation attacking me and demanded—*demanded*—that Governor Christie Whitman renounce me as though I were Satan, all because some cowardly, vicious editor at *New York* magazine had decided (for the sake of newsstand sales, let's not kid ourselves) that I "hate" blacks.

Now, a little background on my relationship with the good conservative Republican governor of New Jersey. Like everyone else, I didn't take her 1990 run against Bill Bradley for the Senate seriously. I felt she was a sacrificial lamb who ran only because nobody else would. However, in one debate in particular, she was quite impressive. She got my attention, and she even got good response in the media, and that's really saying something, because every single news outlet in the state of New Jersey is a left-wing, knee-jerk, Democrat-supporting rag.

When the election came that November, I was told by someone who was at Bradley headquarters that Bill Bradley was "crapping [to quote my friend, and I'm cleaning it up a little bit] in his pants," because the results were coming in and it looked like Christie Whitman was going to pull off the upset of the decade. It was only when they brought in the urban votes from Newark and Camden and Irvington and East Orange that Bradley won.

And the *reason* Bradley nearly lost to Whitman is dramatized in a framed photo that hangs in my office. It was taken in July of 1990, right after Flim-Flam Jim Florio, then governor of New Jersey, foisted his infamous tax grab on the good people of my state. A huge anti-Florio rally was held in Trenton, with thirty-five thousand people in attendance, and I was the main speaker. In November of 1990, the resentment toward Florio was taken out on Bradley, and that really is why he almost lost. Had the Republicans had more confidence in Whitman, they would have put some money into the campaign, and she probably would have knocked Bradley out of his Senate seat.

By the time 1993 rolled around, I was so eager to beat Flim-Flam Florio that I would have supported any of the three Republican candidates. The candidate I backed in the primary actually lost, but once Whitman had the nomination, I wasted no time in throwing her my full support. I made a speech at the Sheraton Hotel in Princeton before twenty-one Republican county leaders, and the theme of my talk was the need for unity, that we must put our past differences aside and rally around the victor.

I then quickly became involved in her campaign, to the point where I was hammering Florio every single day on the air. As a matter of fact, in an interview with a Philadelphia newspaper he said something to the effect of "How can I win with Bob Grant beating my brains out every day?" I kept reminding people of the arrogance of Florio's big tax grab. I also introduced Mrs. Whitman at events at the Reo Diner on several occasions and at big rallies elsewhere. I campaigned for her more than I had campaigned for anybody—ever.

Why did I go so far overboard? Well, I lived in New Jersey, and I felt that Florio must not be rewarded with a second term. I felt that if he won, Democrats everywhere would say, "Aha! We can raise taxes and not have to pay the price." I felt it was a very important message to send nationwide. I also believed that Christie Whitman had all the ingredients, all the qualities, to be a good governor. She appeared on my show several times during that campaign. That's how deeply I believed in her.

And sure enough, right after the election she publicly thanked me and said that without my support, she didn't think she could have won.

Flash forward to less than one year later. I'm sitting in the studio when I get a call from a reporter with the *Asbury Park Press*. He asks me, "Did you hear what Governor Whitman just said in response to the black ministers' rally?"

I said (but only to myself, thank God), "Those so-called ministers must be high on drugs to think that Governor Whitman would *ever* consider selling me out!"

To him I said, "No, tell me." And then he read me her famous quotation:

"While Bob Grant has never used offensive or inappropriate language while I have been on his radio show, I am disappointed if he has begun to use his influence over the airwaves to promote hate or bigotry," she said. "Consequently, I have decided to decline any future invitation to appear as a guest on Mr. Grant's show."

*Well I'll be . . .*

He asked for my reaction. All I could say was that I was deeply hurt. That I couldn't believe it. I said, "She's treating me like an old pair of shoes—use them on a rainy day, and after the storm is over, you throw them in the trash." I realized something important at that moment, that even though I've been around for a long time, I'm a naive, idealistic individual. I was naive enough to think, *Oh, she wouldn't say that—she couldn't say that!* Because, after all, I was a big supporter, and I helped her get elected governor.

But she said it all right. The next day, there it was in black and white: every major newspaper in New York City, New Jersey, and Philadelphia carried her statement. In effect she was saying, to the ministers and anybody else who hates my guts, "Yes, you're right, he is a racist, and now that he's been exposed for what he is, even I, who had been supported by him, am going to distance myself from him." And what her words did was escalate the controversy and give legitimacy to the allegations of the black ministers.

After she spoke, the floodgates really opened—right on my head.

Now look, I'd been criticized before.

But this was the first time it was *orchestrated.* First there was a magazine that decided to build circulation by libeling me and distorting me in the lowest way imaginable. I realized why the photographer wanted me wrapped in the WABC banner—because when you saw the picture, the banner was reminiscent of a Ku Klux Klansman's robe. Then some ministers who had been after my scalp for years saw the opening and took advantage of it. That led a craven neophyte politician who once needed me to decide it was expedient (and safe, now that she was in office) to distance herself. And with that official act, every hack newspaper columnist and blow-dried TV reporter scrounging around for something to fill a slow news day started feasting on me. It was wounded-lion-versus-the-hyenas time, and guess which role *I* played?

Surprisingly, *The New York Times* was very fair in its coverage of the controversy. There was a black reporter from *Asbury Park Press* who was also fair. I did have support—columnists like Michael Myers, who is black, by the way, and Ray Kerrison, Scott McConnell, Eric Breindel. I've always gotten publicity, but never before were there editorials defending or attacking me. I mean, *editorials.* I was sharing space with Bosnia and the national debt. I always said we've got to stop being afraid of name-calling. Too often, a politician or a journalist takes a position for which he's branded a racist, and suddenly he's destroyed, and everything he says is suspect. And I've always said we have to get over being neutered and immobilized by the racist label.

Now the joke was on me—because, lo and behold, this orchestration takes place, and I'm practically destroyed by it. The calls and letters and attacks grew louder and more virulent every single day. This whole thing had me feeling like I had committed some crime, because every day I was asked, over and over and over again, the same thing: "Well, what did you *mean?*" Finally it got to the point where I said that I was not going to do any more interviews. As you can imagine, instantly this mess dominated every minute of my four-hour daily program. It was as if nothing else in the world were going on. But it had yet to get *truly* horrible.

So when did it hit bottom? Was it the day in the middle of this maelstrom when I went to visit my mother in her nursing home, near Chicago, and even *she* said, "What's this I hear, that there was a magazine story and now all the blacks are mad at you?" She's ninety-one and not in the best of health, and I knew she'd feel very bad if she heard the whole story. So I said, "Gee, Ma, I don't know what the heck you're talking about. I'll have to check it out." I sidestepped the thing. But my poor son, who lives on the West Coast, saw the magazine, and he was flabbergasted and very worried by it.

*That* was bad. But not bottom.

Was it when, exhausted by my travails, I begged off attending a "George Pataki for governor" rally in Borough Park? I went home that night and watched a report from the event on Channel 2, and I heard this so-called political editor announce over the air, "Notable by his absence was radio talk-show host Bob Grant, under siege for alleged racist comments. His name was scratched." And later people said to me, "Oh, they canceled you, how terrible." And I had to tell them, "Nobody did any such *thing!*" Even an assemblyman she interviewed on the air said that they wanted me there, but I couldn't make it. But for all the world knew, I had become an instant pariah.

*That* was certainly a terrible moment. But it wasn't bottom.

Maybe the lowest point came on election night, early in November, when Gabe Pressman, who's a classy guy, first asked me to come on the air to discuss the election results, and then called to cancel my appearance, saying that I had become such a story myself that my expertise was now beside the point. When I hung up after that call, it hit me that my life and my professional reputation, which I had spent decades building and nurturing, had been ripped out of my control and damaged, maybe forever.

Believe me, I felt pretty low that night. But that wasn't the lowest it got.

Once the attacks began in full force, I can't say I was totally surprised by them. After all, liberals and anarchists are my natural enemies. That's why I decided after a while not to give any more interviews. They only fueled the fire. Then I got a call from a man named Dennis Prager. You may never have heard of him, but he is a fairly conservative fellow with a TV show based in Los Angeles. He and I even share the same manager. So when Prager called and asked me to come on his show, I agreed. He was a colleague, after all, and if anyone could sympathize with what I was going through, he'd be the one.

My understanding was that we were going to discuss the thing as two colleagues—you know, "Hey, Bob, how do you feel about all this ruckus?"

So we're on the air. He's in his studio in Los Angeles, and I'm in my studio in New York. He begins by holding up the damned magazine cover and then proceeds to recite the slanderous charges against me exactly as they were made: "He's called blacks savages! He's done this! He's done that! Bob—what do you say about it?"

It was a rare moment for me—I was at a loss for words. I said, "What do I *say* about it? My God—do you want me to plead guilty right now?" I said, "Good heavens—I didn't know you were going to do *this.*"

Then—*then!*—he introduces a germ named Walter Fields, at the time an official of the New Jersey NAACP and the man who probably has more genuine hatred for me than any other human being in the world today. Over and over in the course of that broadcast, Fields said he was going to get me off the radio. Finally I said, "Well, look, you want my head on a platter, so what's the point of my saying anything?" It was a total and complete hatchet job. Dennis Prager is a son of a bitch and a snake. Because only a snake would do what he did.

It's hard to imagine anything worse than being on that show that night.

But the absolute, rock-bottom, lowest point in this entire catastrophe came—no surprise—at the hands of a good, enlightened, benevolent liberal politician, Senator Frank "Lousenberg," or Lautenberg, as a dwindling few still persist in calling him. He was at that time running scared against a Republican challenger who had my support, a fellow named Chuck Haytaian (more on him in a minute), and was as desperate as a cornered rat. Lousenberg launched his television ad campaign with a commercial showing his opponent's picture accompanied by these words: "Chuck Haytaian—he's against a woman's right to choose an abortion. Chuck Haytaian—he's against gun laws which would keep assault weapons out of the hands of dangerous people. And Chuck Haytaian is associated with racist Bob Grant."

And then you see *my* picture.

The thought that a creep like Lousenberg was trying to capitalize on my troubles nearly drove me crazy, but that wasn't even the worst part. The worst part was that they aired the spot for the first time during *Monday Night Football.* Which just *happens* to be broadcast on ABC, the same company that owns my station and pays me my handsome salary.

My general manager, Don Boloukos—a good guy, a fair guy, but nevertheless, a guy with the responsibility of running a radio station—brought a tape of the spot with him to a meeting at ABC corporate headquarters. Now, most people who run broadcasting outlets, radio or television, are scared stiff. They're afraid of negative mail and of negative phone calls and of the FCC and of the other media. They're afraid of *everything,* except money and ratings. I think if I had had a typically feckless, pusillanimous program director, I would have been fired in a second.

The upper echelon of ABC, naturally, wanted to know what the hell was going on and why was a United States senator campaigning against a talk-show host who happens to work for them? Thank God I had John Mainelli and Don Boloukos supporting me, because when that meeting was over, I was still standing.

I'll never forget John. When Don Boloukos was discussing the ad up at corporate headquarters, I said, "Well, John, you know the history of Bob Grant and radio stations . . ." (I was thinking about having been fired from another station in town years before.) "Knowing that, it would be much simpler for them to just fire me. And that's probably what they'll do." John said, "Well, I don't believe they will. But if they do, I will walk out with you, and we'll go someplace else and make more money."

I wasn't fired, but Lousenberg wasn't through with me, not

nearly. He remembered how in 1990 I almost caused Bradley to lose his Senate seat, and he knew I was going to hammer him like I did Florio. Lousenberg at that time was chairman of the Senate Appropriations Subcommittee on Transportation, which controls subsidies to Amtrak. And so he wrote to Amtrak's head, telling him to stop advertising on my program: "Mr. Grant has repeatedly made statements of the most hateful and bigoted kind," he lied, to provide a reason. With that, Amtrak pulled its ads.

That grabbed the headlines again, and before you knew it, the "Boycott Bob Grant" movement was off and running. Soon I knew I had really arrived—Jesse Jackson and Al Sharpton held a press conference outside the station. Their point, they claimed, was not to get me off the air or abridge my free speech. Oh, no, they insisted, they only wanted to get my sponsors to drop me. Well, well—is *that* all? We sent a reporter down to Seventh Avenue, and offered them an opportunity to talk to me. They refused to talk.

You know, this is what these people do. I mean, this is their life: demonstrating, conducting boycotts, riding buses around town in the middle of the workday. Whether they really believe what they say in their heart of hearts, I don't know—no one knows—but that's beside the point. This is what they do. I broadcast, you sell insurance or fix plumbing or program computers, and they demonstrate. It's a career.

Anyway, before long my advertisers started to hear the rumblings and calls for my head. Many called my bosses, who were rock-solid in their support for me. Thank God, most of my advertisers stayed with me.

But many business people aren't so brave. Other companies—big sponsors—caved in. One call and that was it. One of them in particular was getting more leads from my show than from any other, and yet this son-of-a-bitch coward canceled. I won't name him, in deference to the rest of the station, because he's still doing business with them. It's so funny. Because mine is the number-one-rated show in its time slot, my ad rates are higher than most. But when the station said, "Look, we'll run your spots on another show," the sponsor said, "But the other show doesn't have Grant's ratings." So the station had to give him *two* spots on another show for every one he had bought on mine.

In all, quite a few sponsors dropped my show. And who suffered most? I continued to draw my normal salary. The station took a hit, but it's a big company, and no stockholders starved. The people who suffered were the men and women who sell ads. Men and women who work hard to put food on the table and keep their kids in sneakers and schoolbooks were the ones whom the demonstrators really *did* hurt. But that's how it goes—that's what these militant, self-styled dictators end up doing. Do they care? Not that I can tell. *They* don't work for a living.

All these travails contained a lesson for me. It was this: If you hold out against the bad guys, you will win an important victory. You will prevail.

Oh, yes, I can say that with a straight face now. Because during this disastrous period in the life of the Republic, something good happened, too.

First of all, the mail. I have never, in my entire career, had more mail, in sheer volume. I have never, in my entire life, had more expressions of passionate, fervent support—thousands and thousands of letters. I never realized the depth of feeling my listeners have for me, and that was a big help. There was some negative mail, sure, but only a very small amount. The negative was outnumbered by the positive maybe twenty to one. The mail said, "Hey, Bob—if they get you, then all is lost." I am perceived by many people as the only guy in the media today who is really telling it like it is. And a lot of people were afraid that I would *stop* telling it like it is. And they were cheering me on in their letters like they never had before.

In the middle of all this horror, I actually got to the point where I was uncomfortable about going out. I began to feel like I had some disease. Then, one night I was going to meet someone at Pal's Cabin, out in West Orange, New Jersey—a very popular restaurant frequented by politicians. And who came over, very eager to see me, but the former governor of the state of New Jersey, Brendan Byrne. The liberal Democrat Brendan Byrne. And he said that he felt bad about what was going on, and he was writing an editorial in *The New Jersey*

*Law Journal* criticizing Lousenberg for forcing Amtrak to drop sponsorship on the show. And, sure enough, a few days later the editorial ran. They called it "Crossing the Line."

I was especially wary of how black people I knew (and strangers, for that matter) were going to handle having to deal with me. And then an engineer at the station by the name of Carl Kush threw his arms around me, gave me a big bear hug, and said, "Bob, I feel *terrible* about what they're saying about you. Believe it or not, I was in Mexico when this whole thing broke, and I heard it on a Los Angeles radio station. I said, 'What are they saying about my pal?!' You don't deserve that."

Vincent, the head of our mail room, marched up to me one day and said, "Hey, buddy—you ain't no racist. I know the phonies from the real people, and you're a real guy." And I don't think these people were giving me any baloney. Paulette, our publicist at the station, had *tears* in her eyes because of what it was doing to me. You know, blacks are very perceptive about how whites react to them. They can spot these phony whites who pretend they're big liberals. I think they have more respect for a person like me than some guy who's kissing their asses. And those blacks who know me personally—and there aren't that many, I'll be candid—know that I treat them with the same respect I treat whites or anybody else.

Everybody I work with was magnificent during my crisis. I will never forget that. That's why I made a vow that I would never publicly criticize any of them. And that includes that diehard liberal Lynn Samuels. I've told the audience, "Don't ever expect me to criticize her, because she stood up for me when I was under siege." I'm the type of person who doesn't cry when something bad happens. But if somebody shows me compassion when I need it, that chokes me up. And that was the only time I ever broke down on the air, the night I said that I will never forget what my colleagues did in standing up for me.

There were other moments of triumph in all the misery. Hurt as I was when Governor Whitman sold me out, I did not condemn or denounce her on the air. It's uncharacteristic of me to turn away from a battle, but I did so for good reasons. I felt that she was still a better choice for the state of New Jersey than anybody who might someday run against her, that her tax-cutting philosophy was still important. And I didn't want to put myself out on a limb by saying a lot of nasty things about her when later I might have to eat those words.

But I know for a fact they got around five thousand letters at the governor's office after she made her statement. These letters were written by people from all walks of life, but a lot of them were very eloquent. And they were all from people who felt betrayed by the governor, people who felt that her turning on me was the same as turning on *them*.

And on November 17, 1994, she changed her mind and returned to my program. How sweet it was. What I think happened is this: When the ministers staged their rally, she panicked, or her aides panicked, and they said, You'd better cut this guy loose right away. Then, when they realized there were more people pro-Grant than anti-Grant, she reversed herself. I have no illusions.

Anyway, she came on the show and said time and time and time again what a huge influence I was, what an important person I was. In the course of the interview I said, "Well, Governor, why would anybody allow themselves to get so concerned over what a talk-radio host would say?" And she said, "Oh, Bob, you're a very important person"—over and over again.

When Senator Lousenberg attacked his opponent, Chuck Haytaian, by attacking me, a funny thing happened. Haytaian, who had avidly sought my backing in the election, suddenly turned tail. He, too, cut me loose and refused to come on my show. And he had been on it quite a bit, back when he thought I could do him some good. He evaporated, you might say. Well, when election day rolled around, Chuck Haytaian lost. There was a Republican runaway train in November of 1994, but Chuck was not on board. They left him standing on the platform, sniffing back tears and waving good-bye. I still like Chuck. I'm sorry he didn't have the courage to stand by me when it counted.

There were a couple of guys who *didn't* shun me during my persecution. George Pataki is one. He's the governor of

New York today. Dennis Vacco is another. He's the attorney general. Jim Treffinger didn't run away. He's now the Essex County county executive. Every politician who stuck by me won his election! Just so you don't think I'm prejudiced, I even supported a Democrat running last fall, Carl McCall (who just *happens* to be black). I announced my endorsement of him back in September. He never joined in with the angry mob attacking me. In November, Carl McCall won, too.

Anyway, like I said, I'm a hero today, but I had to go through hell to become one. I've had number-one ratings periods before. Consistently, I've had good ratings—otherwise I wouldn't have lasted. But this was an extraordinary time even for me. During this crucible, my phones were lit up from the minute I walked in until the minute I left. I never had to give the phone number. It's quieted down some now, but I'd never want to go back to that time, because it was truly terrible—even for a guy who's been in a battle or two in his life and maybe even liked it now and then.

You know, it's a funny thing. Before all this ruckus I would occasionally say to myself, "What the hell's going on? I don't get any publicity. Everything is Limbaugh, Limbaugh, Limbaugh. I was here long before he was. I was a conservative when it wasn't fashionable. And every time you turn around, he's a national obsession. When am *I* going to get some attention again?" And then I got some, more than I wanted. Now I don't mind being anonymous. Make that *slightly* anonymous.

# Ten Great Black American Heroes

——— ◆ ———

1. *Roy Innis*—A highly underrated intellect with a firm grasp on what's really wrong with our society. He's been at it longer than just about anybody, but once he deviated from the party line, he was marginalized by the liberal media.

2. *Thomas Sowell*—Without question one of the most brilliant thinkers and analysts in the U.S. today. His writings on economics as well as on race and ethnicity never cease to dazzle me with their clarity and wisdom.

3. *Clarence Thomas*—If only because he put a lump in my throat and brought tears to my eyes when he nobly defended himself from what he rightly described as "a high-tech lynching."

4. *Michael Myers*—A columnist and conservative who has held true to his principles and demonstrated great courage along with intellect. During my trying times over the *New York* magazine cover, he publicly defended me and my right to be heard.

5. *Joe Clark*—The famed tough-but-fair former New Jersey high school principal. If you've been in a public school lately, you'll know what I mean when I say there should be a Joe Clark running every school in America. A valiant man.

6. *Emanuel McLittle*—The publisher of *Destiny,* a magazine for the black striver class, whose core beliefs in family and

personal responsibility are the strongest and wisest I've ever heard. A spellbinding speaker.

7. *Colin Powell*—The living embodiment of the good warrior—he opposed our involvement in the Gulf War, but that didn't stop him from waging it magnificently.

8. *Muhammad Ali*—I interviewed him once and found him to be a genuine, intelligent, independent guy. A caller tried to bait him into bad-mouthing America, but Ali said, "No, no—I love this country. This is *my* country."

9. *James Meredith*—He served mainly as a symbol when he walked into the University of Mississippi back in the sixties, and maybe he was even being manipulated. But he was truly his own man, a brave one, too, and he believed in the basic goodness of America.

10. *Nelson Mandela*—He's not an American, I know, but I can't list my heroes and not include him. Of all the heads of state in the world today, he is the only one who deserves to be called a *statesman*. His conduct since he was released from prison and elected president of South Africa made the white pro-apartheid leaders there look shabby and small. His dignified, generous spirit is what brought justice and international respect to his country. A true hero.

# I

# American Suicide

———— ◆ ————

*You see it every time you turn around—America is pulling itself apart at the seams. Too many of us are turning our backs on this country's founding ideal: that of many people, one is formed. Once upon a time, we saw ourselves as Americans first, and anything else second. Today, we have a plague of divisions—ethnic, racial, even sexual—that are disuniting the United States. If we had some common enemy, would we put aside our differences then? Maybe an excess of security and comfort are to blame for the dangerously divisive impulses we now so blithely indulge.*

# *Pride and Prejudice*

— ◆ —

I'M AN INDIVIDUAL. MAYBE YOU ARE, TOO.

When I do something right, I expect I'll get the credit for it. When I do something wrong, I know I'll get the blame. You too?

Likewise, if somebody else eats a great dinner, I don't taste it. If somebody breaks his leg, I don't limp. If another man hits the Lotto, I can't go out and spend the money. These would seem to be simple facts of life.

But I know a guy—he's got a wife and two kids and a life of his own. He's got a good job in radio, but one that will never bring him glory. And when the New Jersey Devils, his favorite hockey team, wins a game, he brags, "Boy, *we* showed 'em." When the Yankees rout another team, he says, "Man, we won big tonight." He's never scored a goal or hit a homer, but it's all *we, we, we.*

Now, it's understandable when sports fans do this, and there's no harm in it. But what happens when people think this way about their ethnic group or their religion or their gender or sexual persuasion? When your skin color or ancestry becomes your *team?* In moderate doses, I suppose it's okay—*if* you really need to be proud of something over which you had no control. But when it turns into a preoccupation, it becomes an obstacle to progress. It stops people

**21**

from worrying about their own achievements. It promotes divisiveness and tribalism. And it sends a wrong, damaging signal to the politicians.

Because I'm of Italian ancestry, I could decide to take pride in the fact that Antonin Scalia is doing such a great job on the Supreme Court. I could feel better about myself because Joe DiMaggio was such a magnificent athlete. I could even reach back all the way to Leonardo da Vinci and take some second-hand credit for his greatness.

But if I do so, then don't I also have to bask in the blame owed Italians who were not so wonderful? Shouldn't I also invoke the names of Al Capone and Albert DeSalvo, the Boston Strangler, and even, perish the thought, Mario Cuomo? I should indeed—*if* I'm going to be honest. But the current view of ethnic pride has nothing to do with honesty or integrity.

For instance, nobody objects to blacks saying, "I'm proud to be an African-American!" Nobody begrudges similar expressions by Asians, Latinos, or any other so-called minority. Women are expected to take pleasure in the accomplishments of other women, and here in New York there's even a gay pride parade.

But try telling people you're proud to be white or male or Christian or straight, and see what happens. The Reverend Al Sharpton and Gloria Steinem will lead the protest march right through your living room. You can't have it both ways—ethnic pride is either good or bad. I say it's bad.

I know people of high achievement, winners of Pulitzer Prizes and every other kind of accolade. The one thing they all have in common is that *they* did it—alone. When they were hunched over their novels or their test tubes or their textbooks or their business ledgers, they couldn't pick up the phone and summon the help of every other person in their ethnicity. Achievement is a lonesome grind.

And most people know that. Yet, they persist in this irrational, illogical behavior. Bill Cosby has hundreds of millions of dollars. Are blacks better off because of that? Michael Jordan makes several million a year. Does he split it up among people of his race? No. And why should he? It's his money. He got it because of his talent and hard work.

It's obvious to me what's behind all these expressions of "pride." What people are really saying is this: "I'm not ashamed to be [fill in the blank]! I don't feel inferior just because I'm a [fill in the blank]!" Which is well and good—nobody *should* be ashamed of what they were born. But what kind of person goes around chanting, "I'm not ashamed! I'm not inferior!"? That's an easy one—somebody who's trying to convince himself or herself. Because if you are truly *not* ashamed, if you truly do *not* suspect you are inferior, it will never occur to you to say so.

Shame, of course, is a strong human emotion. It's something that politicians are only too happy to exploit.

The current exploitation of shame and pride began during the civil rights movement of the fifties and sixties. Politicians pandered to the desire in people to feel good about their own group. That's when tokenism became popular. They'd appoint a black or a Latino or a Jew and parade that person around, as if to say, "Boy, aren't I great? Don't I really love you? Aren't you just so happy you can vote for me again soon?"

I get idiots who call and say, "Well, we've got a long way to go, because there are only seven women in the United States Senate!" They don't care about whether we have *good* senators. Only female ones. The same is true of other so-called minorities. And once they get their *paesans* in office, they stop devoting any thought to what exactly those office-holders are *doing.*

That makes the politicians happy—it takes so little to satisfy their constituents. Give a minority some token appointment and everybody's content. How about passing some good laws? Nah, why bother? Nobody cares about that stuff.

The final dishonesty of our thinking about ethnicity is that while people will ascribe good qualities to members of their own group, they are mysteriously silent on the subject of bad qualities. Even mediocre ones. Truth is, for all their whining, the ethnic pride crowd has absolutely no problem with stereotypes—as long as they're feel-good and flattering. It's pathetic.

I, personally, have never been a fan of any stereotypes, good or bad. They offend my idea of how an intelligent person thinks. They're easy labels designed for people with lazy brains, and so I hate them. I believe I'm smart enough to think without them.

My opinion of stereotypes, however, doesn't mean that I don't have thoughts about ethnic groups. I see how people operate, I observe common traits and similarities, and I respond to what I see.

Now, before I get into this, a few words of explanation: I am the first to admit that I (along with everybody else in the world) am more comfortable with members of some groups than others. In my part of Chicago, the West Side, I grew up surrounded by Jews, Greeks, Poles, Germans, a few Lithuanians and Scandinavians, and the Irish. My father had an orchestra, and many Jews played in it, so I've always been at ease with Jewish people. As a kid it never even occurred to me that they were any different from us. Their religion meant about as much to me as their height. In my early days of radio, I was collaborating on a script with a fellow named Milton Maltz, now a giant in the business. And we were arguing, and I finally said, "Milton, you're an egotistical creep!" He said, *"What* did you call me?" I said, "You heard me."

"You know," he said, "that's the first time a *shagitz* ever got mad at me and didn't call me a 'lousy Jew.' " But I didn't think he was acting like a Jewish creep—just a creep.

And because as a kid I knew so many Poles, I never understood why Polish jokes portrayed them as stupid. They seemed as dumb or smart as anybody else.

But I knew no blacks during my youth, and that, I think, accounted for my view of them as foreign and forbidding. The same is true of people from the Third World. I'm not as comfortable with them as I am with white ethnics. Does that mean I think that all Asians and Africans and Latinos are bad? No, not at all. It's not their fault that I feel as though they're unknowable. I'm sure I seem strange to them.

Now, then.

I know a great many Greeks, and they are a fine people— hard workers, warm, responsible, and all-American. But they are absolutely scandalized if a Greek wishes to marry a non-Greek, and that disturbs me a little. Why do they fear outside influences? What do they think a little American blood will do to their culture? For some reason, the Lebanese and Armenians I know remind me of Greeks. They, too, are usually fine citizens and likable people, but they also hate the idea of intermarriage. I don't see what all the fuss is about.

Koreans are hard for me to pin down. Back in the early eighties, I used to work near a dilapidated, rat-infested, crummy, vacant storefront. A total eyesore. Then, I noticed it begin to change. There was hammering going on, sawing, painting. And, over a period of time, that dump became a gleaming white fruit and vegetable store, all thanks to the Korean family that had worked night and day, breaking their backs, to build an attractive business that thrives to this day. Nobody gave them anything. They didn't mug anybody. They erected a monument to the American dream.

And yet I find Koreans very difficult to know. They are tough, I have no doubt. That's why they survive. Still, I wonder where they're going as a people. Whether they really want to become full-fledged Americans. Probably, they do. But for all their numbers and their success, they haven't really made the effort to give something back to American life, either through public service or politics or any other visible endeavor. They remain outsiders.

I find Italians exasperating. They have contributed so much and have so much more to offer, and yet they are cursed with an inferiority complex that holds them back. They are the most self-demeaning people, as a group, that I've ever known.

I've known and loved Jews since I was a kid, but sometimes they can be vexing. If they're your friends, they're extremely loyal. But if they're out to get you, look out. With good historical reason, they're tenacious and tough. But they are far more skeptical and uneasy about Christians and Christianity than Christians are about Jews and Judaism.

Hispanics are tough to consider as a whole, because what is a Hispanic? A Mexican? A Puerto Rican? A Cuban? Yes to all the above, though those groups are far from interchangeable. It's only our own stupidity and myopia that leads us to bunch all these people under the single heading of "Hispanics." They certainly don't see themselves as one people.

Cubans I have known seem no different from most people of European ancestry. They're industrious, hard-working, and intelligent. That's why they could not tolerate Castro— Cuban-Americans are entrepreneurs and go-getters, exactly the wrong kind of people to live under Fidel's rule.

When I lived and worked in Los Angeles, I got to know some Mexicans. They were devoutly religious and had rock-solid, responsible family values. I had an engineer, Don Collardo, who was a terrific guy. I remember that when I had taken a job in New York, he said to me, "Hey, a word of advice: Be careful of those Puerto Ricans."

And I was shocked, because I had more or less lumped Mexicans and Puerto Ricans all together. I said, "Don, why do you say that?"

He said, "Oh, the Puerto Ricans have ruined that city."

Since I've moved here, though, I've had the good fortune to meet many Puerto Ricans. Like Mexicans, they are religious and family-oriented. I have no problem with Puerto Ricans. So there goes another stereotype, shot to hell.

I *do* have a problem, however, with what I'll call "professional Hispanics." These are the people of Latin American or Caribbean background who, for political reasons, insist that they are a single ethnic minority deserving of special treatment. They're the ones who want bilingual everything to spare them the trouble of having to learn English. They're the ones who want advantages at work and school just because they have Spanish names. They cry discrimination and we foolishly kowtow to them, without even understanding who they are or considering whether they have been mistreated.

I'm still of two minds about the Japanese. When I was in Japan, I found the people to be polite and well-behaved. The teenagers there don't inflict graffiti on their cities, and they show respect to their elders. Japanese-Americans got a raw deal during the World War II internment, but they bounced back and became hard-working achievers.

But unlike the Germans, the Japanese have yet to accept the blame for their monstrous actions at Pearl Harbor and during World War II. There's something frightening to me about a national character that allows for such evasiveness and dishonesty. And until they really come clean, I will have reservations about Japan.

When I was a child, Chicago was a strictly segregated city—the white ethnics here, the blacks there, and almost no mingling. When I would go visit my grandma Teresa, she would say, in Italian, of course, "Now, don't go to Claremont Avenue—the blacks are there." People used to say, in effect, "Gee, you know, if it weren't for the blacks, everything would be fine. We'd have a nice melting pot where everybody more or less gets along."

Then, as time passed, the black neighborhood began to migrate west. "Uh-oh," someone would say,"they're up to Western Avenue." "They're up to Kedzie Avenue." And so forth. Every block they occupied was another block off limits. And that was the world in which I grew up.

In recent years, I've gotten to know many black men and women. Some, like Thomas Sowell and Walter Williams, are great intellects, towering figures whom I admire. Others are just normal people—good, decent, hard-working folks who defy every negative stereotype you can throw at them. It's a cliché, but only because it is so true, to say that there are good people and bad people in every group.

What some people perceive as my problem with blacks is in fact my problem with how race has been politicized, mostly by whites. To constantly say to a group, "Yes, we've abused you, we've enslaved you, we've treated you as second-class citizens, and therefore we will now trash all our notions of fairness and grant you special favors" is ridiculous hypocrisy. It glorifies and perpetuates victim status. It rewards helplessness, and to reward a behavior is to encourage it.

Look, imagine that a bunch of politicians and pundits and professors told you over and over that the odds are against you and you'll never succeed without their help. After a while, *you'd* believe it, too. But who gains from you believing such a thing? Not you, that's for sure.

I'm also against giving Indians special favors. You know, I was born in this country, and according to my dictionary that makes me a native American. So how did the Indians come to be the only ones to deserve that label? Again, we can't go on making excuses for people based on something that happened hundreds of years ago. Who gave Indians the right, for example, to operate gambling casinos? What kind of favor is that? Absurd.

There were many Indians, who, prior to all this madness, strove to be good Americans. There was even one, a Navaho named Ira Hayes, who helped raise the flag on Mount Suribachi, at Iwo Jima. But then the politicians in Washington said, "Hey, wait a minute, we just discovered that you're not merely Americans. You're Americans *plus."* Well, I don't recognize "Americans plus."

Recently, I was operated on by a gastroenterologist who came here from the country of India. He's an urbane, intelligent, skillful surgeon and physician. And although I respect him and I'm grateful for his expertise, I still wonder, why does it appear that so many of our doctors and people in the medical profession are from India? What happened to the American doctors and medical professionals? What's going on here? This is not meant to fault the Indians who come here, although there's one big problem I do have with them— I am allergic, deathly allergic, to curry.

Now, the one ethnic group with whom I've had more trouble than any other is the Irish. Being an Italian kid growing up in the city of Chicago, I knew a lot of Irish people. And because of my fair appearance, many times they mistook me for Irish. And I would notice that once my playmates' parents heard that my last name was Gigante (which it is, in case you didn't know), their treatment of me would change a little. As if to say, "Oh—one of *them."* I was well aware even as a child that the Irish and the Scandinavians held Italians in low esteem.

There was an Irish kid by the name of Eddie Egan who used to call me "Jew Ganti." Now, I was a pretty good little fighter even back then. My Uncle Joe Colucci had been a boxer, and he taught me how to box and got me a pair of boxing gloves. I was deceptive, because I was small and I was a pretty good student, and kids tend to think that if you do well in school, you're a sissy. A lot of guys picked on me. And they all got surprised.

Well, this Irish kid, Eddie Egan, called me "Jew Ganti" over and over again. I'd say, "Why are you calling me that?"

He'd say, "Because you're a Jew." That in itself was an insult in his mind. I would say, "No, I'm not, I'm Italian." And he'd say, "Well, that's just as bad."

Finally we had it out. He was bigger than me, but I gave him a fat lip and a bloody nose. I mean, I pounded him. He's swinging at the air and I'm working him over.

That night, I'm up in my room, doing homework, when the doorbell rings. I hear my father calling me downstairs, and when I get there, I see Eddie Egan's father in the house.

He looks down at me and says, "Did you beat up Eddie today?" I said I did. Well, you could tell by the look on the father's face that he was surprised by what a little guy I was. His kid had a swollen nose and could hardly talk. I didn't have a mark on me. I think he was a little embarrassed.

After the guy left, I tried to explain, but my father whacked *me* around. When high school graduation time came, my father attended the ceremony, and I said to him, "Dad, remember that kid I beat up? Well, there he is." And my father saw this guy who towered over me. "Why didn't you tell me he was so big?" my father asked. "I tried to, Dad, but you wouldn't let me say anything."

He was a typical Italian father—worried to death about what other people would think. Most often, the Italians were afraid it was the Irish who were looking down on them. A terrible way to go through life. No wonder that before long, you began to see expressions of "Italian pride."

And you know where *that* kind of thinking gets us.

# How the Third World Wages War Against Us

— ◆ —

IMAGINE, IF YOU WILL, THAT TWO HUNDRED AND TWENTY OR SO years ago a bunch of Maori tribesmen came to North America and founded a nation here. Or imagine that a boatload of Chinese peasants did it, or some Arabian bedouins, or a tribe of Zulus or Mayans or Eskimos.

What kind of country do you think this would be? Do you think we'd have free elections, a system of governmental checks and balances, a constitution to ensure that the minority isn't oppressed by the majority? Do you think we'd have a founding document that guarantees us freedom of expression, of religion, of due process under laws that are applied equally to all?

Do you believe this country would have fostered awesome advances in science that make human life safer, easier, and more enjoyable then ever before?

Do you think such a nation would today have a glorious history of more than two centuries as a beacon to freedom-loving people all over the planet?

In other words, do you think you'd recognize it as America?

If you answered yes, please put this book down, go take your brain medicine, and sit quietly in the corner.

This country works as it does for one reason only—it was

formed by the genius, ideals, philosophies, and efforts of eighteenth-century European men. They were the heirs to the most highly advanced political, intellectual, and social culture in the history of the planet, and that's what they brought to this land. All our beliefs about freedom, about the rights of the individual, about equality of birth in the eyes of God, about the role of law to keep the peace—they came from western Europe and nowhere else.

Good thing those brave, wise men didn't try such a stunt today! Imagine if a group of contemporary straight males of European ancestry attempted to create and lead a new nation—I tell you, they would be treated as though they were committing a crime against nature. Picture the outcry from all the non-straights, non-Europeans, and non-males (all of whom, by the way, enjoy greater freedom here than anywhere else in the world): "To the gallows!" they'd screech. "Chauvinist, racist, elitist pigs!" Lucky thing the world wasn't such a sophisticated and benevolent place two centuries ago.

Not convinced yet of the main source of America's blessings? Okay, then look at any other spot on the globe—Asia, Africa, the Middle East, the southern hemisphere. What do you see? Tyranny. Tribal uprisings. Anarchy. Repression of the many by the few. Revolving dictatorships. Revolution. Murderous religious warfare. Class warfare. Race warfare. Civil strife. Officially sanctioned slaughter. Guerrilla death squads. Juntas left and right. Military strongmen who are here today, standing before a firing squad tomorrow.

I have shoes that are older than most of the governments that run the Third World today.

America is unique in the history of nations, thanks to the men who gave birth to it. If you still don't believe me, try this *(please):* Go away. Emigrate somewhere else and live there for a while. Pack up and move to Saudi Arabia or Japan or Guatemala or Nigeria. Do you think they'll bend over backward to make sure you have every damn street sign and election ballot and official form and textbook in your own language? Will they strive to allow you to preserve all your customs and traditions the way you like them? Will they provide you with food stamps and a comfy little stipend just

31

for breathing, the way we do here? Ha ha ha. Don't forget to write (if your new homeland has a working postal system).

Our glorious beginnings just make the crisis now gripping the nation all the more tragic. Never in the history of the world has any civilization set about, in a seemingly methodical way, to destroy itself. Until, that is, the greatest civilization on the face of the earth, the United States of America, began to do just that in the latter half of the twentieth century.

We weren't always so foolish. For quite a long time, we had an immigration policy that favored the ancestral lands of this nation; mainly, western and northern Europe, meaning Great Britain, Germany, France, Ireland, and Scandinavia. Then the policy was broadened to allow immigrants from southern and eastern Europe, which accounted for the influx of Italians, Greeks, Poles, and central European Jews. Even though they were diverse, they still had a common European heritage and culture. There were always immigrants from Asia and elsewhere, but most newcomers to America were European. And everything seemed to work well. As a matter of fact, I think it's safe to say, it worked miraculously.

But then along came 1965, and with it, a bloated, besotted individual I have nicknamed "The Swimmer." He is known to you as Senator Edward Kennedy of Massachusetts. It was his legislation, introduced in the United States in 1965 and signed with alacrity by Lyndon Baines Johnson, that changed not just the immigration laws, but also the face of America and, I am afraid, the future of America, too.

The main characteristic of this legislation was self-destructiveness. That a skunk like Teddy Kennedy would seek to promote self-destruction is perfectly understandable to me, and even welcomed, as long as he kept the damage to himself. But he went much farther. His legislation mandated that no longer would European immigrants be given any kind of preference. Quite the contrary, the new law overturned the national origins quotas that favored Europeans who wished to come here. Thirty years later, where do the majority of newcomers originate?

That's right. In the Third World. The so-called "developing" world. From Africa. From Asia. From Latin America and the Caribbean.

Now, you can make the argument that an immigrant is an immigrant, and it shouldn't matter to us where they're from—that they're all created equal. To which I say: Nonsense. Just because our Declaration of Independence says that all men are created equal doesn't mean that, therefore, "all men" have an unalienable right to live in America. We reserve the same right as every other nation on the planet to control our borders and set sensible immigration guidelines.

But thanks to Wet Teddy, we now have an average annual immigration of almost one million people a year. That's *legal* immigrants. Quite a few more than we need. Remember, the great wave of immigration early in this century coincided with a growing economy here that required the labor of millions. No such economic condition exists today, so every nickel in the pocket of a newcomer comes out of the pocket of someone who was already here.

What has been the result of Kennedy's tragic act of self-loathing? Look around you.

The short-term damage due to the current crop of immigrants—uneducated, unskilled, and seemingly unable to become so—is costing us plenty. I just read where they receive at least $16 billion a year in various social service funds. There is a myth that immigrants are contributing taxes in proportion to what they're taking. They're not.

All my life, I've had Social Security deducted from my paycheck. And that deduction was matched by my various employers all these years. Who's benefiting from that? I'm not going to see that money again. Elderly immigrants who have never contributed a dime to Social Security are coming here and receiving SSI stipends. I just read a report about a Social Security program that was defrauded of $40 million by Cambodian refugees in California claiming falsely to be mentally ill. It's a scandal.

But that's just the superficial destruction that immigration is causing to our country. There is a more profound damage that goes far beyond wasted money. By dint of sheer numbers, these newcomers are shredding the fabric of American life.

Once upon a time, immigrants came here and wanted only to be "good Americans." George Washington himself, the father of his country, said that newcomers should become "assimilated to our customs, measures, and laws: in a word, soon become one people."

As the grandson of immigrants, I can tell you firsthand that it used to work that way. I remember my grandmother, struggling so hard to do the best she could. When she came to this country, there were no bilingual programs, there were no food stamps, there was no SSI. There was nothing but the promise that you could make it, if you worked and fit in.

And work she did, having married a man who became an invalid at a very young age. How did she do it? She struggled to adapt to America's ways, chiefly by learning the English language. Sure, she had an accent so thick you could cut it with a knife. We used to have fun teasing Grandma for calling the legendary Arthur Godfrey "Ar-tura Godfield." But that didn't stop her. And there was something else about my grandma. Maybe your grandma, too. She loved the United States of America. No matter what regard she had for her Italian roots, she was proud to say, "I'm an American." And, indeed, she was.

I know lots of Greeks who have emigrated only recently to America. But as soon as they settle here, they are Americans first. They work hard to learn English and insist that their children speak it as a first language. They don't lose their love for their ancestry, however; in fact, they send their kids to after-school programs to learn Greek as well as English.

The Jewish community is another great example of people becoming American yet not losing their roots. They, too, send their children to after-school programs, to make sure they learn Hebrew as well as English. The Jews never made excuses about discrimination, though they suffered greatly from anti-Semitism in this country. Despite the bigotry that sometimes hounded them, today Jews have the highest per-capita income of all ethnic groups in America. They didn't ask for special treatment. They didn't bitch and moan because somebody didn't like them. They ignored all the obstacles and soon prevailed.

But that's changed. Nobody's coming to America to become

American anymore. They're coming here to set up their own little enclaves, exploit the local economy, and send the money back home—like colonies, or better yet, like parasites. They don't pay taxes or serve in the armed forces or join the PTA or volunteer at the Red Cross. They don't care about the American way. They barely know what the words mean.

And sadly, we, as a people, have given up on insisting that they try their hardest to become Americans. Too many of us have lost our confidence in this great nation, and so we no longer champion its ideals. That's why I say that the future of America as we have known it is over.

Look at Queens, for example, a place I lived back in my early days in New York. When I first arrived there, in 1970, it had enjoyed a long history as a multicultural paradise, home to Italians, Poles, Irish, Jews, blacks, you name it. Everybody coexisted because they were all Americans first, and proud of it.

In Queens today, you can't tell which country you're in. The store signs are in Korean, Chinese, Urdu, Hindi. You're not quite sure where you are—Seoul? New Delhi? Karachi? Port-au-Prince? Taipei? The rage for bilingualism has wiped out even the idea that Americans share a common language. And if we can't speak to each other, *are* we one nation? What would happen today if we faced a great peril, like Hitler or the Japanese in the forties? Would we be able to band together, put our minor differences aside, and fight the foe who sought to destroy us? When I look around, I can't imagine that we would.

The multiculturists say that it's immoral and hurtful to suggest that the American way is better than any other. They'll be happy when the Asian-American way, the Latino-American way, the African-American way, the Female-American way, the Homo-American way, and last (and least) the Euro-American way all enjoy equal standing. They'll be happy when this country resembles a Tower of Babel with no central culture, no backbone, holding us all together.

Now, I realize that some people prefer to live with myths. The current comfortable lie is that America has always been multicultural and that diversity only makes us stronger. Total nonsense. I don't think that diversity is a magic spell that always improves the quality of life. At a certain point, it just becomes chaos.

And as we permit the steady, quickening dilution of western European culture that created this country, we're losing the country itself. Just as our American forebears did, these newcomers bring with them *their* idea of how life should be lived. *Their* idea of how differences should be settled. *Their* idea of civil rights and personal freedom and privacy from the interference of government or religion or any other outside force. Then where will we be?

I have no idea. I can guarantee you one thing only—it won't be America.

There's a certain irony in the fact that while lots of people believe this in their gut, they're afraid to come out and say so. We were told this republic was founded to escape the brutality of King George, who would brook no disagreement. And now we're right back to that—living among tyrants who allow no alternative viewpoint. People can no longer express a true sentiment if its runs counter to the worldview of the P.C. Police. The more diverse we've become as a people, the less free we've become as a nation.

If we were honest, we would all admit this fact of human nature: *Nobody* wants to be in the minority. Not in any situation of any kind. And especially not in their own homeland. In Nigeria, Nigerians wouldn't stand for that. In Korea, Koreans wouldn't stand for that. In Argentina, Argentinians wouldn't stand for that.

Why on earth would *we* stand for that?

Once, a few years ago, a caller quoted a story from the front page of that day's paper claiming that thanks mainly to immigration, white New Yorkers were now in the minority. And he wanted to know how I felt about that.

"Well, it doesn't make me happy," I said. "After all, I'm white. Why *should* I be happy?"

Would you be surprised to hear that my response made news? And not good news, either—for stating an honest emotion, for daring to sound like a normal human being, I was criticized and beset and besieged. "Hate Radio," screamed the front page of one of our fair city's tabloids, and before long the rest got in on the act. It got so bad that I was called to a meeting "uptown," meaning at ABC headquarters on Columbus Avenue. Some of the network brass wanted to ask me a few questions.

So we all sat down—me, my station manager at the time, and two ABC execs. The big exec held up the papers. "You know," he said, "we like publicity. But we don't like *this* kind of publicity." And I said . . . well, what the hell could I say? I just shrugged. *I* didn't ask the papers to quote me. Finally, the guy said, "This quote here, this quote doesn't look good."

And I said, "Well, *why* doesn't it look good?"

He said, "You know, you're saying, 'I'm white and I don't like being in the minority in New York.' "

I then said, "Look, give me some guidance on this. Because, if I were a Haitian radio announcer and I said I was glad so many Haitians were coming to New York, nobody would complain. If I were a Korean announcer and I said it, nobody would complain. Why would it be okay for *them* to celebrate outnumbering *us* and not the other way around? I didn't put down any other group. I didn't say Asians are no good, Latinos are no good."

Silence.

My point is this: We don't need to apologize for wanting America to stay recognizably American. And that's the best, final reason for stopping the flood of aliens who have no intention of assimilating themselves into American life. It's *our* country. We *built* it. We *paid* for it in sacrifice, blood, and toil. If foreigners want to come here, it's got to be on *our* terms from now on. Not *theirs*.

If we were smart, we'd immediately cut back immigration to no more than one hundred thousand newcomers a year. And we'd encourage Europeans first, just to even out the damage of the past three decades of free fall. Our population is already too big at 265 million. We should adopt a policy of zero population growth, at least until we've absorbed all the immigrants we've taken in, legal and otherwise.

We've also got to do something about the illegal immigrants. They now total roughly three hundred thousand a year. The liberal softheads like to weep and beat their breasts over these poor creatures. I have begun to think of them in a different

way. They're like soldiers come to invade us. Their countries
of origin could never hope to defeat us militarily and plunder
these shores for our riches. So, in despair, the illegals cross our
borders and pick us to pieces, like hyenas on the carcass of a
gazelle. We don't even try hard to stop them. We can't even
agree that we want to. In the end, the difference between them
and an enemy army's assault is that they make us bleed dollars,
not blood. We have to protect our borders from illegal aliens
the same as we would from armed troops.

But what's that you say? How are all those poor foreigners
supposed to live in freedom and peace and prosperity if we
won't let them move here? Well, it's not my job to solve
their problems, but since you ask, here's a suggestion, free
of charge.

If they love the American way so much, let them recreate
it wherever they live now. Let them adopt a constitution like
ours and establish the universal right to vote, and a congress
and a supreme court and everything else. Let them allow
capitalism to flourish. If they're as good and smart as us—
and they *insist* that they are—they'll have paradise on earth
in no time at all.

But no, they can't do that. They never quite explain *why*
they can't, but they can't. All they can do is insist that they
have a God-given right to come here and bring along with
them all the savagery, poverty, pestilence, ignorance, and
tribalism of their homelands.

It's as though your poorest, sorriest, most ignorant neighbor
heard that you have a beautiful home, a real garden spot—
and instead of building his own, he decided to move in with
you! Would you stand for that? If you did, how do you think
your home would look after a week or two? Would it still be
a showplace?

Well, of course, you'd never allow him in the front door.
But we, as a nation, have no problem letting all our poorest,
sorriest neighbors move right in with us. I don't blame *them*
for wanting to live here. I blame *us* for being such dopes and
patsies that we let them.

I've said this over and over: America will not fall because
our enemies are so *strong*—it will fall because we are so
*weak*.

# *Happy Columbus Day*

———— ◆ ————

NEUROTIC, PSYCHOTIC, GUILT-RIDDLED WHITE-LIBERAL SELF-LOATHING springs up at you every time you turn around, it seems, but then there's the one day of the year set aside to actually celebrate this mental disorder, a day that is to pale-faced self-abasers what Mother's Day is to Mom. I'm speaking here of October 12—Columbus Day. Or, for those of you with short memories, what some now call Indigenous Peoples' Day or Discovery Day (which sounds kind of like Christmas without Christ).

If you know anything about Christopher Columbus, you know he was a brave and great man of vision. They weren't even his ships, but he took them beyond the limits of where European man had gone before. He could easily have given up on his quest, but he did not. As a result, he made a great discovery. One that the entire world, but we Americans in particular, has benefited from.

Were there men and women here before him? Yes. And they created a life here, to the best of their ability and desire, until Columbus ushered in centuries of European domination. Granted, that may not have been what the Indians wanted, but do you wish you grew up in *their* idea of America? Columbus and those who followed tamed this continent, and then they made it into the land of liberty. What would the Indians have done with it? Would they have made it a place where the oppressed people of a hundred countries could go to find peace and prosperity?

We honor Christopher Columbus because he discovered the land where we built this monument to human freedom. That's all. And no one can deny that without his first step of exploration, America could not have happened.

But now Columbus has been vilified and villainized. I have read essays that blame him for all the ills that followed his discovery; they wail that if it weren't for him, great Indian civilizations would be flourishing, that all he did was enslave the Indians, those whom he didn't murder. His holiday has been muddied by crybabies who hate everything that is European and civilized. No one claims Martin Luther King, Jr., was a saint, but his holiday is right up there with Christmas in the eyes of some.

Well, no one claims Columbus was a saint, either. But he did what he did, and it was a staggeringly good thing, a necessary thing, and if he doesn't deserve a holiday, then neither does—Mom.

# What Do Women Want?
# (Don't Ask)

——— ◆ ———

As is typical of mankind in the latter half of the twentieth century, we have gone from one extreme to the other when it comes to the sexes. There's been no stopping at some fair middle ground: we've gone from a world where women truly were second-class citizens—and undeniably, they were—to where they now enjoy a status above that of men.

Oh, the feminists *say* they want nothing more than equality. But they also say they deserve special favors and privileges denied to the less-fair sex. They *say* they deserve to be heard just as men are. But they also insist that meeting *their* needs is now civilization's top priority. They *say* they want an end to the sexual double standard. But then they insist on protection from nasty male appetites.

In other words, they're completely confused. They can't handle getting everything they asked for. Not that there's anything new in that—even Freud finally threw up his hands and asked, "What do women want?"

Here's one thing women undeniably want: Virtually all of them—feminists, old-fashioned girls, doctors, lawyers, and Indian chiefpersons—still want to be married and have babies. This much we know.

But they even manage that in a confused way. Just look at the feminist name game.

41

The beautiful and desirable Miss Johnson—pardon me, *Ms.* Johnson—decides to marry lucky Mr. Murphy. Oh, she'll *marry* him all right, but will she take his name? Not on your life. In lots of cases, she'll adopt the cumbersome fad of hyphenation. That slender little hyphen barely connecting the partners symbolizes all the tension evident in today's version of domestic bliss.

Anyway, the day will come when Mrs.—oops—*Ms.* Johnson-Murphy brings forth a little one. I believe the custom is still for the child to bear the father's name, which reveals the complete sham behind the game. For if modern woman is so intent on keeping her surname alive, why not demand it be passed along to her children?

But wait—maybe that day is coming soon! Then Ms. Johnson-Murphy's child will be known as, oh, let's call her Jessica Johnson-Murphy. She'll grow up and someday meet a fine young lad by the name of Jason, the offspring of Mr. and Mrs.—sorry—*Ms.* Jackson-Duffy. And Jason and Jessica Johnson-Murphy-Jackson-Duffy will live happily ever after.

Until, that is, their son Harry becomes a man and falls in love with the lovely Miss—dammit—*Ms.* Zoe Martino-Goldberg-MacDougal-Chang.

Why do women want to break the centuries-old tradition of taking the man's name? Because they're been taught to see adopting his name as *giving in* to him. And who has taught them that? Women who see men not as mates but as *competition*. Women who want to turn every contact between the genders into a contest, a wrestling match, a struggle of wills. As a result, every place where men and women come together—the kitchen, the nursery, the office, the bedroom—has been turned into a battleground.

And how do these feminists justify their declaration of war? They promulgate the myth that men don't like women. That we believe we're better than women. Now they even have convinced themselves that men *fear* women.

What a load of hooey. No normal man fears women or thinks they're inferior. We never did. Women are not better than men. They're not worse than men. They are different from men. The differences are clear to any six-year-old, which means that to your average overeducated nitwit, they seem somehow uncertain, obscure, and evershifting.

The feminists started out by proclaiming that people should be treated all the same, regardless of gender. Today everything on their agenda involves treating women differently—much *better*—than men are treated.

For instance, the libbers screamed loud and long for the right to do any job a man can do. They put up a particularly fierce battle to become firefighters. Now, in many cities, the firefighter test required an applicant to carry a two-hundred-pound weight up and down a ladder. Sounds reasonable, considering that the essence of their work is to save people from burning buildings.

But no, the feminists shrieked. Because few women can manage such a feat, the test must be made easier for them. Not for the men, mind you, just for women. They have to be allowed to carry a *fifty*-pound weight. Which means that you'd better go on a diet now, just in case you ever have the misfortune to be slung over the back of a dainty female firefighter.

Feminists started out demanding sexual equality and the freedom, in the clinches of romance and lust, to dress and speak and do exactly as they wish. Soon, though, they began trying to force males to *stop* doing exactly as *they* wish. And so today's young men, instead of conducting themselves in the way nature drives them to, must now adopt more gentle and feminine approaches to seduction. They must first *ask,* "May I touch you here? Oh, please, if it's no trouble, may I fondle you there?" If you neglect to ask first, you'll be decried as a rapist and run off campus like a criminal. How did "freedom" bring all this lunacy? Because the feminists declared that women *are* different and must now be treated like sensitive little flowers.

As I started by saying, women want to *have* children, but too many have decided they no longer want to *raise* them. Too much trouble, not enough fun. Not enough *power.* Besides, men don't do it, so how valuable can it be?

Now, before I go any further, I want to state clearly that the following does *not* apply to women who *must* work. And there are many of them. Divorce, illegitimacy, and an uncertain job market make it impossible for some women to stay home with the children. That's regrettable, but understandable. Better they work than go on welfare.

But once the feminists got to work, they bemoaned all the seniority and years of experience that worked to the advantage of men. What's the cure? Work long and hard paying your dues, as men have done?

Hell, no. Declare yourself a "minority"! Never mind the technicalities—namely, that women are actually the *majority* in America, and *men* the minority—because words only mean what we *tell* them to mean. And "minority" no longer carries the dictionary's definition. It now is merely a label used to justify giving complainers anything they demand. "We're a poor little minority; therefore, we need special advantages!"

That can mean only one thing—affirmative action! Which has provided negligible help to blacks, who are at least a genuine numerical minority, but has been an enormous windfall to coddled white middle-class females.

Are they happy yet? Ha ha. The mean, nasty men at work say rude things to them. They stare at their bouncy parts and act like . . . *males.* The nerve of them! Forget that men have been intimidating and harassing other men on the job since time immemorial. Women need special protection! They're too delicate to tell some jerk to back off or lose his hand. They're too fragile to put that bully in his place. They no longer remember how to employ a well-timed slap in the face. No, while every other kind of harassment is okay, *sexual* harassment is illegal.

Now, telling a woman, "Put out or get out" is wrong and *should* be outlawed. But the laws go much farther than that. They say that if a woman says she's been made to *feel* "uncomfortable," then she has been harmed. The laws practically make it illegal to be rude to a woman. And if men are sometimes rude, then the laws will make it illegal to be men!

So, thanks to affirmative action and sexual harassment laws, women can comfortably join the American workplace, right? But the poor kids at home are cutting into her time that could be spent climbing the corporate ladder! Okay— turn Daddy into Mommy, slap an apron around his waist, and force him to watch the tykes. I'm just waiting for the medical treatment that will allow men to breast-feed—then women will go right from the delivery room to the boardroom. Bringing men into the delivery room was just the halfway measure, I am convinced. Before we're through, pregnant men will have their feet in the stirrups, and their mates will be standing by, coaching them on how to breathe.

But until then, let's force Daddy to pony up for a nanny. Let's get some illegal alien who'll work for peanuts to raise the kids. So what if little Junior and Sis end up speaking with Spanish accents? They'll fit right into twenty-first-century America. Our most urgent problem is too many children being raised by lousy parents or no parents at all, and the solution to this as proposed by normal middle-class adults is to encourage even more unloved, uncared for, insecure children than ever.

But Mommy still isn't satisfied. She doesn't want to spend her hard-earned bucks on day care. How can she and Daddy do that and still afford two vacations a year? Well, that's easy enough to fix—make the taxpayers pay for it. Let's take a federal government that's on the verge of economic collapse and force it to provide free day care to anybody who wants it.

All this turmoil, all this courting of catastrophe, for one reason only—because *some* women insist on "having it all." They insist on saying from one side of their mouth that there's no difference between the sexes and from the other that there's *plenty* of difference.

And why do they do that? Because they're women!

# Why Some Men Are So Screwed Up

───── ◆ ─────

Maybe we should be grateful to whatever social movement it was that made it all right for Bob Dole to do publicly, openly, and unashamedly what cost Ed Muskie the Democratic nomination for the presidency just twenty-two years earlier.

Muskie, you'll recall, was running an exhausting campaign for the party nod in 1972. He was drained, mentally and physically, by the time he got to New Hampshire for the crucial primary there. Both he and his wife had been bitterly attacked in the pages of the *Manchester Union-Leader,* the state's famous right-wing paper. In the middle of a press conference called to answer the attack, standing outside the newspaper's office, he made his fatal mistake.

He began to cry.

After that little outburst, he was immediately declared null and void by the political pundits. Any man who cries in front of the press *must* be too unstable to run the country, the unspoken opinion held. Instantly, he lost his spot as the front-runner. In fact, for him the race ended there.

Flash forward to 1994, to the televised funeral service for Richard Nixon. Senator Robert Dole is delivering his eulogy.

He begins to cry. But no one is shocked or disquieted by his outburst. Nobody questions his political future. Hardly anybody even notices. And at this writing, he is the front-runner for the Republican presidential nomination.

It seems like men generally feel easier about crying these days. It has never bothered or embarrassed me. I tend to cry at certain movies, mainly during portrayals of compassion. *Brian's Song* was a real tear-jerker for me. Even *The Philadelphia Story* merits a tear or two.

I cry in a masculine way. Not with great, heaving, tearing sobs or moans and groans. I cry silent tears. But not imaginary ones—real tears. I am asked to deliver eulogies from time to time, and I never get through one without crying.

It used to be that men who cried were called cowards or fairies. They were thought to display a feminine inability to control their emotional responses. I believe it's better to show an emotion than squash it.

Does that make me more sensitive? I have no idea. I feel as insensitive as ever. Does it mean I am more in touch with my feelings? I don't think so. Men have always felt grief and sadness, whether they cried or not.

I mention all this in light of the sad state of masculinity today. Feminism's outrageous, unnatural demands have always included the one that goes, "Oh, if only men could cry and show their feelings and express what's deep inside and begin to see how women must feel when they *blah blah blah . . .*" I think it's a lot of nonsense to suggest that only if men act like women will they be complete human beings. But it's a brand of nonsense that seems to have caught on in America, at least. The feminist leaders and lesbian activists want to turn men into women with the ability to produce sperm. They don't *like* men, you see—they don't like the way Father Nature made men to behave.

Now, women have *always* had their differences with men. These complaints about men being nasty, violent, animalistic, grabby beasts are nothing new. And it is only the difference between the sexes that keeps romance alive and kicking.

But these harpies have completely politicized the ways in which men and women differ. Women's ways are good for society, they insist, and men's are bad. And they use their whiny propaganda to wipe out masculinity wherever they find it. It's gender McCarthyism—"Are you now or have you ever been a member of the Testosterone Party?" If you answer yes, you're a criminal.

I'm not talking about all women, mind you, or even most. But it doesn't take many shrill voices to make trouble. Plain and simple, I'm blaming the likes of Gloria Steinem and Betty Friedan. What we used to call *libbers.*

Weak-minded men have responded to their pressure by going in one of two directions, neither of which is healthy or sane. Some take all the male-bashing seriously and allow themselves to be neutered and emasculated. These wimps buy the nonsense that their own natural male instincts are destructive and evil. They feel guilty about liking to look at women or about wanting to take them to bed. They feel ashamed of their own energy and aggressiveness and competitiveness. White men, in particular, seem vulnerable to this. Their sex *and* their skin color have been so demonized, it's a wonder they haven't committed suicide en masse.

The other destructive male response to feminism is to go in the other direction and become *anti*-female. Instead of caving in, these guys become abusers and wife beaters or rapists and serial sex-killers. "I can't compete with you at work," they say, "so I'll beat you at home." There have always been men who hit women, it's true, but I think that today more men than ever fear the loss of their masculinity. Nothing can justify or excuse this kind of criminal behavior. These jokers belong in jail, just like every lawbreaker. But let's at least recognize that it is partly a response to something external.

Look what feminism has done to flirtation and seduction, the very forces that brought each and every one of us into being. It used to be that men propositioned women, and women reserved the right to say yes or no. It may not have been perfect, but it *worked,* I can tell you.

No longer, though. Today we have terms like "date rape" and "sexual harassment" for what used to be just red-blooded male desire and courtship. As I've said, forcible sex is a crime that should be punishable by the death penalty. And telling a woman at work, "Put out or get out," is wrong and illegal. No one feels more strongly about that than I do.

But today a woman can give in to a man, think better of it the next day, and claim she was "pressured" into having sex. Not physically *forced,* she'll concede. Not *blackmailed,* certainly. But he said words that magically took away her freedom to choose: he somehow talked her into it, or he whined and pleaded all night, and she didn't have the gumption to kick him out. The next morning, she cries date rape.

And the current definition of "sexual harassment" has nothing to do with coercion either. If he says or does something that makes her feel "uncomfortable," he is now guilty of harassment! Let me say that again: For these delicate little flowers, discomfort in matters of seduction equals harassment! You don't need evidence. You don't even need to prove his motive for making you uncomfortable, because no motive is necessary. You just have to say you felt "uncomfortable," whatever that means, and he is guilty in the eyes of the world.

No wonder some men wimp out on sex these days!

I'm glad I'm not a young man today. Some things are easier (the young women, especially) than when I was a kid. But other things, like knowing what it is to be a proud, masculine male, are more difficult. Too many young guys have no idea of who or what they *are.* No wonder today so many men are crying.

# Some Straight Thinking About Gays

——— ◆ ———

HOMOSEXUALITY HAS BEEN WITH US SINCE DAY ONE, AND TO DENY that or to insist that it's some modern social ill is absurd.

Scientists are still trying to figure out why some people are homosexual and others are not. But one thing is clear to me: It's not a choice. It's not a lifestyle decision. You don't wake up one morning and say, "You know what? I'm tired of vanilla. From now on I want . . . *tutti-frutti!*"

I have known homosexuals in my life, and through work, and I have had no more problem with them than with anybody else. Some were nice guys; some were jerks. They were all human beings, and they deserve the same respect as you or I. Live and let live, I say. As a matter of fact, a fellow who was my friend told me one day that he was sexually attracted to men. That was the beginning and the end of conversation on the subject. I never had any problems with him as a result, and he never had any problems with me. As long as he didn't turn sweet on me, what did I care whom he went to bed with?

One thing most homosexuals I've known had in common was this: They were all on the unhappy side. There was nothing "gay" about them. Common sense will tell you why—*nobody* wants to feel like an oddball. Human beings want to feel special, but they also want to feel normal. Considering how much shame we feel about sex in general, it's hard to go through life as a sexual outsider, I imagine.

The wisest way to handle it, then, would seem to be by calling as little attention to it as possible. Most people don't devote much conversation to their sex lives anyway, so it should be easy. The best policy here, as in so many instances, is to do what you want and mind your own business.

And the vast majority of adults, gay and straight, would be happy to handle the matter of sexual preference in that way. What prevents us is how homosexuality has been politicized by a rabid few. The extremists have made it into just one more so-called *issue* that adds to the divisiveness already infecting American life. (By the way, that's one word I wish we would strike from common usage. Today, *everything's* an "issue." Race, sex, religion, you name it—what were once normal parts of everyday life are now *issues* to be seized and argued and contorted and manipulated. Whenever I see the word, I know I'm about to lose my temper.)

So *who* is responsible for turning what we do in our bedrooms into an issue (oops!) requiring debate, lawsuits, and legislation? Blame the nuts of the Christian right and the nuts of the Godless left. They did this to us. We're all in the middle somewhere, ducking their bullets.

The Christian zealots are wrong when they say homosexuality is a sin and a crime to be wiped out if possible. You can't do that without wiping out homosexuals. The Bible waggers are wrong to say homosexuals shouldn't hold certain jobs, such as teacher, for instance. There have been homosexual teachers since there have been schools, I guarantee you, and nobody minded before. There's a danger that heterosexual teachers could seduce their students, but we don't ban straights from working in schools. We just make strict rules and keep an eye on things, and it works pretty well.

But the Godless nuts of the left are just as wrong when they turn everything into a fight over "gay rights." Homosexuals deserve the same rights as anybody else when it comes to jobs and so on. But this new cry for *special* rights is unfair and damaging to society as a whole. It turns sex into one more thing that keeps us from behaving like a single nation.

Here in New York, homosexuals have been wailing about

their "right" to march in the St. Patrick's Day parade. Believe me, homosexuals have been marching in that event since it began. They marched as Irish men and women—same as the straights did.

But that's not what the gays want now. No, they want to march in a parade honoring a Catholic saint under banners glorifying a practice the Church abhors. They lie when they say they want only to march down Fifth Avenue. What they want is for the pope to announce that from now on homosexuality is wonderful! That's the "right" they're truly demanding. And whether you agree with the official Catholic position or not, we all have to allow the Church the right to its own opinion. You don't like what the Church says about you? Find another church.

Marriage has always meant one thing and one thing only— the union of a man and a woman, usually with the intention of bringing children into the world. Nobody stops homosexuals from vowing to love one another forever or from living together. They can wear long white dresses with veils and carry little pink bouquets, for all I care. But that is not a marriage! Rather than live with that fact of life, they now want *marriage* to change to accommodate their wishes.

Because certain practices, homosexuality among them, seem to be the way the AIDS virus is transmitted, it *should* be fairly easy to stop. Today, every schoolchild knows how to prevent the spread of AIDS. And one way is through contact tracing—using investigators and mandatory reporting to find and treat people who may have been exposed. We've been aggressive with that method of tracking sources of tuberculosis and syphilis. So why not AIDS?

Not on your life, the activists say. No, the stigma all you nasty heterosexuals would bring down on people with the virus is too terrible to bear—even worse than a deadly epidemic. That means people will continue to die. Even the gay virus enjoys special rights denied to other viruses.

The professional homosexuals and their sympathizers have got our lawmakers so cowed and intimidated that they're afraid to stand up for the rest of us. When the activists don't get their way, they fling around their version of the racist label—they cry "Homophobia!" What nonsense! We're not *afraid.* We just want our nation to be as sane as possible.

It's no different than everywhere else in American life today—a few hardcore complainers have seized the power to make judgments about how the rest of us think and live. It used to be okay to scorn homosexuals, to treat them with disdain and even contempt. That was stupid and wrong, and most people no longer feel that way. But the extremists won't be happy until they can freely abuse and vilify heterosexuals. They won't rest until they've taken every advantage we're foolish enough to allow.

# More Rights from the Left

———— ◆ ————

Any time you hear the word "rights" being used, what the speaker is usually saying is this: "Most normal people are bad. They're insensitive, stupid, selfish, offensive, and hurtful to anyone or anything that is not a normal person. And so the majority need to be kept in line—they need to be physically restrained and morally corrected."

Now, why would *that* get my goat?

The worst part is that these rights "activists" attach their neuroses to genuinely reasonable ideas. Nobody can defend bigotry or prejudice. Nobody wants to destroy nature. Nobody is in favor of cruelty to animals. Nobody wants to keep disabled people from living their lives to the fullest. And we have laws that embody those beliefs.

But that's not enough for the rights crowd. Deep down, they hate the people they condescendingly think of as "normal." They feel superior to humanity itself. They believe it is responsible for every bad thing on the planet, starting with civilization.

So they claim to speak for the trees. For the minks. They identify a little too closely with the inanimate and the dumb, to the point where they begin to insist that a tree has the same "rights" as a person. And therefore, it deserves the same kind of treatment. They actually believe that trees and

54

beasts are *superior* to people. But they'll settle for equality in the eyes of the law.

The big cry in the animal rights movement is this: "A rat is a pig is a dog is a boy." In other words, a rat has the same rights as a person. Touching. But why stop there? Why isn't a cabbage a rat? Why isn't seaweed? Algae? Moss? They're all living things, too. What about equal rights for bacteria?

These activists won't be happy until we all kill ourselves. Because everything we do is a conflict with some other living organism's so-called rights. Let's stop eating meat, vegetables, and fruit. Let's not cut down any more trees to build houses. Let's dismantle civilization, which has, by their thinking, violated the rights of every living thing on Earth.

The radical activists for the disabled are only slightly less nutty. They want the disabled to take part in normal life, which is fine. But their idea of normal life is one where disabilities have no bearing on what a person can and cannot do. A lovely fantasy, but completely disconnected from reality.

The Americans With Disabilities Act of 1990 *sounded* high and mighty, but it was yet another misguided liberal attempt to legislate the facts of life. In essence, it attempted to make any recognition of disability illegal. The insanity here is that the majority is expected to shell out billions to allow a small minority to enjoy its "rights." The National Association of Counties has said that county governments alone will spend $3 billion to build and remodel facilities to satisfy the law.

In New York, high-tech public toilets were introduced to the streets, a good idea in an age where some people urinate openly, without shame. The contraptions solved a nasty problem with one stroke. Until, that is, the wheelchair brigade started screeching that because their chairs couldn't fit inside the toilet booths, they should be revamped or banished. We could have said, "Look, if you're in a wheelchair, you'll have to plan your life around that. You'll have to pay closer attention to your physical needs than people who can walk do. It's a tough break, but that's life."

But that's *not* what we said. Remodeling the toilets would have been prohibitively expensive, so they were meekly withdrawn. No fully able person sued for the right to public accommodations. Now we're back to barbarism for all. That's equality.

And the law's definition of "disability" was left so vague that it grows daily. R. Emmett Tyrrell, Jr., the columnist, publisher (of the excellent *American Spectator*), and bane of Bill Clinton's existence, writes that the law could be used to protect people with bad breath or allergies to perfume or other imaginary "disabilities." He reports that in L.A., a strip joint had to close its onstage "shower act" because it was inaccessible to strippers in wheelchairs.

The wheelchair radicals must face the fact that they're going to have to adapt without forcing the rest of us into debt. *We* didn't disable them.

As far as animal rights activists are concerned, I wish there were an open season on them, just as we have open season on ducks, deer, bears, and other creatures. If they want to identify so closely with animals, that's what they deserve. I like leather shoes. I like steak. I love to see a beautiful woman in a fur coat. I think it's sexy. Sue me.

# Ten Great American Heroines

◆

1. *Phyllis Schlafly*—Living proof that one woman of conviction constitutes a majority. Due mainly to her bold stand against the masses of feminists and their sympathizers, the Equal Rights Amendment was defeated. She stopped a juggernaut of nonsense, practically single-handedly.

2. *Jeane Kirkpatrick*—As our ambassador to the United Nations, she symbolized the unwavering strength of America on the vital issues of support for Israel and opposition to the Soviet Union's colonialist foreign policies.

3. *Myrtle Whitmore*—She showed fierce independence and courage by working for peace in the Crown Heights section of Brooklyn while others attempted to foment divisiveness and hatred. She also fills in for me from time to time on the radio, just another reason I call her a friend.

4. *Barbara Bush*—Despite her lofty status and high profile, she remains down-to-earth, unpretentious, and human. Because she is secure in who she is, she is able to speak her mind without sounding strident or pushy.

5. *Elizabeth McCaughey Ross*—New York's lieutenant governor has achieved great success as a thinker, author, and politician. But she is also completely comfortable with the fact that she's a beautiful woman and doesn't feel the need to apologize.

6. *Marilyn Quayle*—She is a very smart, disciplined thinker

and a trained professional, but she never competed with her husband like some other ambitious political wench I could name. Mrs. Quayle realized the huge importance of her husband's job, and she saw the wisdom in doing all she could to support him in that.

7. *Midge Decter*—First, only a person with a keen mind and a fine intellect like hers could stay married to Norman Podhoretz. Midge deserves a great deal of the credit for the rebirth of conservatism among educated, intelligent Americans. She was gutsy to fight that battle in the face of elitist, Ivy League liberalism.

8. *Meryl Streep*—She is the most gifted actress of our time, end of story. She submerges her own ego into the role she's playing, like a true artist should. It burns me up to see every little flash-in-the-pan starlet who comes along getting the notice and praise (and money) Streep should be receiving.

9. *Lally Weymouth*—Because she lives in the capital and writes for *The Washington Post,* you'd expect her to be just another bleeding-heart sob sister. Instead, she consistently displays courage and freedom of thought and spirit. Her columns defy the liberals and speak out on behalf of sanity and hardheaded realism.

10. *Mary Gigante*—My mother belongs on this list for a multitude of reasons, not least of which is that she represents a kind of American woman we'll probably never see again. These women devoted themselves to their families and scraped through the genuinely hard times of the Depression, all without whining. All these women wanted was the chance to guide their children into positions where they could take full advantage of all America offers. Without them, *none* of us would have prospered. Thanks, Mom.

# The Making of
# Bob Grant

◆

I WAS BORN A CONSERVATIVE.

My father came here from Naples when he was six, and my mother was born here to Italian immigrants. We lived in Chicago, which was (and is) one of America's great Democratic strongholds. My mother's mother used to kiss Roosevelt's picture, just as she kissed her picture of the pope. My mother's entire family, in fact, were typical New Deal Democrats.

My father *hated* Roosevelt.

He thought the last good Democrat was Grover Cleveland. He believed the Democrats were a bunch of phonies, led by the biggest phony, FDR. My father didn't trust the New Deal or collectivism or socialism or any other isms that were in vogue during the Depression. He also thought Roosevelt was wrong to drag the U.S. into foreign disputes. My father was a great believer in the individual and the free enterprise system.

It's not as though my father was sailing along merrily, financially at least. He was a violinist with a little orchestra, but when people were starving, music wasn't very high on their list of priorities. He had hired a seventeen-year-old kid to do orchestrations for him, and before long the kid had gotten them a contract to go to Hollywood for three weeks.

59

But my father refused to go. "What if we don't catch on?" he asked. "Then we'll be out of work after three weeks." (He needn't have worried. That kid he hired was David Rose, who became a big-time bandleader, most famous for his record "The Stripper.")

So, you see, my father was as fearful of poverty as any staunch New Dealer. He once took a job as a movie theater projectionist to make ends meet. And whenever the newsreel would show FDR, which was all the time, my father would monkey around with the projector to distort the sound. It would suddenly begin to drag in long, unintelligible bursts. He got such a kick out of doing that to Roosevelt.

Both sides of my family are loud, demonstrative, and argumentative. And I remember hearing political discussions—arguments, really—going on all the time. It was always the same—my father against everybody else. He liked being a maverick, I think.

The worst was during the presidential campaign of 1940. We lived in a crowded apartment building that faced other crowded buildings. Back then the fashion was to put a photograph of your candidate in your window. You'd stand outside looking—Roosevelt, Roosevelt, Roosevelt . . . Willkie?! That was our apartment. The only photograph of Wendell Willkie to be found in all of Chicago, for all I knew.

I tell you, I wished my father had placed a photo of FDR up there. No kid likes being the oddball. And Willkie's picture actually caused me trouble. I got into fistfights because of my father's rebel politics. He wasn't hanging around with kids in schoolyards or on the street. *He* didn't have to defend Willkie with his fists, like I did.

One man who saw our window got so mad he wanted to throw a brick through it. My father marched right down and started talking to the man. He said, "You don't believe in this country. You should go to Germany or Russia. In this country, we have the freedom to elect our leaders. What's the matter? Are you worried that Roosevelt won't get *every* vote?"

Our window remained intact, but the incident left an impression on me. Here my father was, simply expressing his opinion, and people who disagreed became violent. What did that guy care whose picture was in our window? Nobody was stopping him from voting for Roosevelt. Still, he wanted to silence any opinion he didn't share.

There's a lot of my father in me, even to this day. I discovered, thanks to him, that by expressing an unpopular opinion, you can expose the true nature of your opponents. That only when people are confronted by voices they don't want to hear do they reveal their truest, innermost beliefs. When I express an outrageous view on my show, I am disappointed if I don't rile *somebody.*

My other great political tutor back then was Colonel Robert R. McCormick, the owner of the archconservative, right-wing *Chicago Tribune.* My father read it religiously, and so did I.

But my father and I were a special brand of conservative. Really, our politics could best be described as right-wing libertarian. My dad knew anti-Semites, but he had lots of Jewish friends and fellow musicians, and was completely at ease with them. I am, too. As a matter of fact, he used to say that he was a *true* liberal, because he believed in live and let live. He never would have understood the religious right or all the fuss about pornography or abortion. He would have said the same thing I say—mind your own business.

He actually thought that Roosevelt was on his way to becoming a dictator—that the NRA (National Recovery Administration) and all the bureaucracies the New Deal created, plus the raising of the income tax, were setting the stage for total government involvement in our private lives and wallets.

By the time I got to high school, I was a professional arguer. I was a member of the student council and the debate team, and it seemed as though I was always making a speech. Many times I was campaigning for some other student's run for school government office. I got a big kick out of helping some underdog win the election. After a while, I acquired my nickname—The Senator. I had become known for being able to mount convincing, statesmanlike arguments for whatever I believed in. My schoolmates started to say that someday I'd represent Illinois in the U.S. Senate. I liked that, I'll admit. There were kids in that school who didn't even know my name—they'd yell, "Hey, Senator," and I'd know they meant me.

But I also had a streak of mischief that would have made me unfit for politics, at least as it's practiced today. Once, I recall, I was walking down a corridor at school, approaching two of my teachers, Mrs. Yetter and Mrs. Pocha. As we passed, I looked up and said, "Hello, Ruby! Hello, Agnes!" I was just being a wiseguy, but they saw fit to reprimand me all the same. Quite a difference from today, when students call their teachers every foul obscenity in the book with impunity.

So that's what made me Bob Grant. But how, exactly, did I *become* Bob Grant?

Flash forward to the spring of 1949, when I was working at WSBC, a little radio station in Chicago. It was a foreign-language station, but they used English-speaking American announcers to read the news and introduce the programs. Just for the hell of it, I got myself an audition at the big CBS station in town, WBBM. I really didn't expect to get the job.

A couple of weeks later I'm at work when I get a call from the other station's operations director. He says, "Bob, we'd like you to come to work for us." In those days we played records for our theme music and whatnot, and at that moment I was standing next to a big stack of disks. And I was so dumbfounded by the call that I knocked over the whole pile, breaking every single record. Flabbergasted. I said, "Well—are you sure you mean me?" I told the people I was working for at the time, "That was WBBM! That was CBS! They want me to go to work for them!"

So I went over to CBS, but there was an immediate problem. Somebody asked me, "What name do you use on the air?" I said, "My name—Bob Gigante." "Oh, no, no, no," he said, "if you want to work here, you have to Americanize your name. We don't want any foreign-sounding names."

I said, "Really?"

He said, "Hey, look—you know Larry Alexander? His real name is Zandrini. Tony Parrish? That isn't his real name. His name is Anthony Parisi. If you want to work here, you come up with a name." I said okay, but before I chose one, I wanted to talk to my father.

So at home that night I sat down with my parents and told them. My father immediately said, "Yeah, that's show business. Everybody uses different names. When I used to play music in some places, I was Pat Geegan and the Orchestra." But he thought Geegan sounded too Irish for me. So we took my name and tried to figure a way to keep the initials. And that's how we came up with Grant. My father had no problem with me losing my name. "What the hell?" he said. "Get the job." The one who really felt bad about it at the time was my mother. She said, "But Gigante is your *name.*" She just felt that it was strange and wrong to drop it. To this day, she regrets that I changed it. But then, you know, it was a different world. People felt completely comfortable about expressing anti-Italian sentiments at that station, even using the word "guinea."

That's why a lot of these multicultural nuts today really get on my nerves. They say, "Hey, white man, you had it easy."

I did?

# II

# Why Nobody Loves
# Free Speech

———— ◆ ————

*Oh, of course you* think *you love it, right? After all, you're a good American, and free speech is a large part of what America's all about. And you do love to speak freely from time to time. It's a good feeling to say what's on your mind.*

*But genuine free speech is always—let me say that again—*always *accompanied by pain. Somebody is always going to have his or her feelings hurt when other people say what they believe or observe or think. And because nobody loves pain, nobody truly loves freedom of speech. We don't have to love it. But we must defend it.*

*Gee, did I hurt your feelings? You'd like me to say I'm sorry? I can't—the pain is the price of freedom. And I'd rather you be free than pain-free.*

# The Biggest Sin of All

———— ◆ ————

THE MOST UNFORTUNATE TENDENCY IN HUMAN NATURE IS, AT FIRST glance, a rather benign trait:

We all want to be liked.

We all desire approval.

We all wish for applause instead of boos. In fact, if half the world is applauding and half is booing, we all try and play to the half that's against us—to placate them and win them over. The danger there is the risk that we'll offend the half that was clapping. But still, being human and foolish, we try.

These efforts make phonies of us all.

Now, some people are rewarded for being phonies. Politicians, for instance. We demand that they be leaders, but they know we're not completely serious. A politician can succeed without ever having to take a strong stand on a single issue. We don't demand that they do or say the right thing. We simply insist they refrain from doing or saying the *wrong* thing—meaning, anything that upsets us. It's a tricky dance, but as long as a politician can restrain himself from telling a hurtful truth or taking a position that reveals a rock-solid but controversial belief, we're happy to applaud on election day and send them back to their cushy offices.

They know this.

I hate this kind of fakery. But I must confess that when I began in talk radio, I was just as phony as all the rest of them.

My earliest contact with radio was, of course, as a listener. I was raised on the CBS network, and my heroes back then were people who today would probably be politically correct lefties: Edward R. Murrow and Eric Sevareid. What impressed me about them was their ability to discuss an issue and sound so objective and balanced and Olympian. You could tell they had a liberal bent, but they were so professional and impassive that you couldn't quite nail them on it. It was all "on-the-one-hand-this-and-on-the-other-hand-that." And because they were my teachers and role models, when I started in radio, I found myself doing the same thing.

For example: There was an election being held in Chile, and in that race were three candidates. One was a right-winger, the second was a moderate, and the third was a two-bit commie stooge by the name of Salvador Allende.

One night when I was on the air, someone called and asked what I thought about the election. And instead of saying what I believed in no uncertain terms, I said, "Well, on the one hand you have a candidate who represents a moderate approach to government; on the other, you have Allende, who represents a more radical approach, but perhaps, in view of the fact that Chile has had economic problems . . ."

A lot of baloney! Chile wasn't having problems any worse than any other country in South America. As a matter of fact, Chile was one of the so-called ABC countries—Argentina, Brazil, and Chile—which then represented the greatest hope for Latin America.

In my heart of hearts, I wanted Allende to lose. But I also wanted to sound above the fray. I wanted to impress the audience with my ability to be as godlike as Murrow and see all sides.

Then we had an election here, in 1964. There was no doubt in my mind that I was going to vote for Barry Goldwater. But partly because of the constraints of the FCC's equal-time provision and fairness doctrine—all that garbage that shackled opinions—and partly because I wanted to sound "professional," I hid my true belief. I talked about how "maybe the

Great Society *does* have something to offer, although Barry Goldwater represents what could be *blah blah blah . . .*"

More baloney! I didn't mean a word of it. As I spoke I was thinking, "Lyndon Baines Johnson is a big fake, phony fraud who's deceiving the American people. He is a liar, and Barry Goldwater offers our only hope for any kind of self-respect." I would have loved to have said that. Had I said it, history would have made me a prophet, because Goldwater said that if we were going to be in Vietnam, then we ought to be there with all our might, while Johnson kept saying, "Ah seek no wider war." And by the time he left office, the number of American troops in that Southeast Asian hellhole had gone from 16,000 or so to 529,000!

If that were today, I would pound LBJ every single day, as hard as I could, and laud Goldwater just as hard. So what did I gain from holding my tongue? Not a thing, except the comfort of knowing that I was no bigger a fake than everybody else in radio.

So, we're saddled with this pathetic human desire to be universally beloved—or, at the very least, to be more or less undisliked. This might be an acceptable foible, were it not for how it impedes our progress and undermines our efforts to solve problems. For our problems are not so huge! They're far from insurmountable for a nation that was born in strife, as ours was. When we've had to, we've overcome all the enemies and obstacles that at the time seemed so strong. But the need to be loved stops us from making the tough decisions and the unpopular but necessary actions to get us back on track. We're no better than our leaders, so we can't fairly fault them for being phonies and weaklings. It's what we tell them to be. We order them to damage no one, and so they end up damaging us all.

They deliver a speech, for instance, and then their pollsters burn up the phone lines to find out how people felt about it. "Oh, gee, you shouldn't have said that about those seagulls causing problems with the airplanes, because there are a lot of bird lovers out there," the pollster reports back five minutes later. "The Audubon Society's going to be mad at you."

*Screw* the Audubon Society! People are more important than seagulls, so get rid of the damn birds now! I'm not inventing this "controversy," by the way. It really happened here in New York City when the birds were interfering with planes at JFK Airport. The animal-rights groups said that killing the gulls wasn't nice. They suggested putting off dealing with the problem until a "humane" solution could be found. But what was so humane about jeopardizing people's lives until then?

Politicians aren't responsible for every problem, however. It's up to us, in our normal discourse, to point them in the direction we want them to go. But we don't have the guts to do it. Instead, you'll hear people who appear to be sensible and rational, people who have found pragmatic, successful ways to run their own lives, suggesting "solutions" that sound ludicrous the second they're uttered. These intelligent individuals spout the most incomplete, illogical, half-baked, mush-headed, mealy-mouthed, starry-eyed, wishful-thinking gibberish—I mean the kind of nonsense that would make Pollyanna snort—when asked their view on some social ill. They'll embrace a solution whose guiding principle would cause them to retch were you to demand that they actually live by it. They'll propose that we behave in violation of everything that common sense tells them, of every truth they know about how human beings act and react. They'll endorse policies for society as a whole that they'd never dream of adopting themselves.

In other words, they'll lie. So everyone will like them.

Look, people conduct themselves falsely when the stakes are almost nil. They'll say you look great when you've gone without sleep for a week. They'll tell you that red dress doesn't make your butt look fat. They'll say you chose the best birthday gift ever. Why, then, if people lie about trivia, would they be any more honest about the critical issues? They won't.

As a result, we've got one of the biggest intellectual hoaxes of all time, a method of thought control more powerful than anything dreamed by George Orwell or Aldous Huxley. Political correctness makes people sound like idiots, and they know it, but they're helpless to stop. It's unnecessary to use behavior modification or mind-altering drugs to control what people think. You can just exploit their desire to be lovable.

Some pious saint announces that, from now on, to think this particular thought makes you an evil human being. It makes you dirt. Do you want to be dirt? Not many people do. Faced with that pressure, it's easy to swallow your words, proclaim that you'd *never* think such a horrible thought, and quietly join the ranks of nice hypocritical people.

It's hard to make your stand and say, "Hey, buddy, who died and made you God? Who gave you the power to label this thought bad and that thought good? I reject your authority!"

It's hard to stand up to tyrants, even thought tyrants.

So the next time you're moved to wonder, "How did we get in such a mess?" the next time you think, "How could we have believed this tactic would solve that problem?" think of this:

We'd rather be loved than right.

# Look for the
# Racist Label

———— ◆ ————

THERE HAVE ALWAYS BEEN CHEAP, EASY, EFFECTIVE WAYS TO SI-
lence people who are saying things you don't want to hear.

In the Middle Ages, Galileo made some surprising astro-
nomical findings, and then Copernicus discovered that the
earth moved around the sun. The Catholic church hierarchy
didn't want anybody to hear or believe any of that, so it
accused them of heresy. That shut them up in a hurry. You
had to speak the party line even though you knew better.
Science was not permitted to investigate and let the chips
fall where they may. Opinions had to conform.

It's the same way today. Nobody worries about heresy any
longer, thank God. These days, heretics are called *racists.*

It shuts them up just as surely as Galileo and Copernicus
were silenced and disgraced.

Am I the only one who wonders why our society has such
a frenzied obsession with racism? I don't mean just that we're
against prejudice, bigotry, and discrimination—I agree completely with that. I've experienced prejudice in my life.
Growing up as an Italian-American who didn't look particularly "Italian"—whatever that means—I've heard lots of
mindless ethnic hate and fear in my time, and it has always
sickened me.

But today, every time you pick up a paper you see the

modern feeding frenzy at work. Every day there's news of some well-intentioned person who questioned the liberal dogma or some hapless soul who spoke rashly without first weighing every word for political correctness. In every case, there's hell to pay.

Now, ask yourself—why does anybody become obsessed with anything? An obsession is an unhealthy fixation. It has deep, disturbed psychological roots. It's my guess that a lot of whites in prominent positions feel guilty, for some reason, when they think about people who are different from them racially and ethnically. Maybe they themselves harbor secret hates and fears. Rather than admit it and deal with it, they scrutinize every word uttered by everybody else. And when their sick fixation leads them to "discover" racism in another person's heart—bingo! The feeding frenzy begins.

The attacks on so-called racism or misogyny or homophobia are constant and relentless, and almost always succeed in destroying their target. The rhetorical term is "poisoning the well"—neutralizing a speaker by questioning his underlying intentions. When you call someone a racist, it means he has a mindless hate for every member of a particular group, and he is unable to be trusted in anything he says regarding them. And so he should be shunned and shamed and go unheard evermore.

It's downright funny. Today, people are willing to extend sympathy, understanding, and the benefit of the doubt to every pervert, junkie, liar, drunk, thief, fraud, deadbeat, or any other kind of lowlife who comes down the pike. You can kill your parents in cold blood and convince jury members that your screwed-up childhood is responsible, not you. You can get away with anything if your sob story is good enough.

But say something that the good, tolerant, freedom-loving liberals don't want to hear, and you immediately join Hitler in the hottest part of hell. The individuals behind these assaults are masochists, I believe, pious, neurotic, guilt-riddled, hypocritical masochists filled with self-loathing. And we allow these sickos to set the public agenda and decide what can be discussed and what cannot.

None of this is to say that racism doesn't exist. It does.

The Klansmen, militiamen, neo-Nazis, and so-called patriots who call for the extermination of blacks are a genuine danger. But they're hardly representative of all white people. They're nuts. Thirty, forty, fifty years ago, we had genuine racism in America. Back then most whites really did not feel that blacks were our equals. There's no denying it. But that's past tense. Back then, I was no better than anybody else where race was concerned. I was no big liberal. I didn't march in any civil rights parades. So what I'm saying applied to me, too. You didn't think about it. Blacks just weren't *there*. You would go to a motion picture, even, and rarely would you see black actors in any role other than maids or porters. So there was a stereotype. And it was damaging.

But that kind of blatant discrimination is not what comes under attack today.

I'm talking here about the person who can't help but notice that affirmative-action programs are inherently unfair to whites and Asians, and he says, "Wait a minute. Isn't *all* discrimination wrong? Isn't it a stereotype to assume that all whites have it better than all blacks?" He gets called a racist.

A black man called a talk-radio program a while ago—not mine—and complained about the coverage of the O. J. Simpson trial and the Colin Ferguson trial and the trial of a murderer up in Westchester County. He said that all three of these stories were being reported solely because the defendants were black. And there are a lot of blacks who have that paranoia—it's totally irrational. How do you deal with it? You cannot debate the point, because they have made up their minds. And it's very frustrating. Didn't this guy ever hear of Ted Bundy or the Son of Sam or the Manson family?

Welfare reform is a big issue today. Even a bleeding heart like Bill Clinton agrees we need it. But New York Congressman Charlie Rangel says that when conservatives talk about cutting welfare, they really mean they want to make blacks suffer. "Welfare reform," he says, is a code word for racism. Rangel says the same thing about this frightening term: "tax cuts." He even thinks that's a code word for racism. (I guess he doesn't think blacks want to keep their hard-earned money out of Uncle Sam's pocket.) Back when Nixon was president, there was a groundswell of support for this term:

"law and order." That, too, was allegedly a code word for racism.

The president of Rutgers University makes a statement that blacks' SAT scores are lower than those of whites. And therefore it's not fair to use those scores to decide who gets into the school, because genetically and environmentally, blacks are not capable of measuring up. He's attacked ferociously. He apologizes. They still want him ousted. He says he didn't really mean what he said, that what he really meant was that black students' disadvantages were responsible for their low SAT scores. That's *still* not good enough. They want his head. No one has yet suggested that we determine whether his original statement was correct or not. The truth might be too scary to live with.

So you can't talk about affirmative action without being branded a racist. You can't talk about crime or the death penalty. Or welfare reform. Or tax cuts. Or college admissions standards. Or immigration. Or genetics. Or out-of-wedlock births, or homelessness, or drug addiction, or AIDS. Everything is a code word. Every subject is forbidden. That's the land of the free and the home of the brave today.

Who actually benefits from this loss of freedom to debate important issues? That's easy—the Jesse Jacksons, the Al Sharptons, the NAACP. As Roy Innes calls them, "the racial hucksters." They will call whatever they're against "racist," and it's been effective in quieting their critics. Why? Because it immediately does two things: It puts their opponents on the defensive, and it gets other whites to condemn them.

Let's face it, if you could utter one little word to silence all your attackers, wouldn't you do so? I'd sure as hell be tempted. The manipulators who cry "racism!" are just being crafty. We're the dopes for letting them get away with it. Their goal is not the eradication of racism. They only want to further their own agendas and line their own pockets.

Think of the National Basketball Association or the National Football League. If you watch pro sports, you'll see that most of the players are black. Why? The coaches will tell you it's because they want the best players. They want to win the game. And it just so happens that the best players are black. Nobody questions that for a second. But what if all the best players were white? Then you'd hear it long and loud—racism! For some reason, it's okay if the entire New York Knicks starting five is black. It if were all white, it would be anything *but* okay. Has Jesse Jackson called for proportionate representation of whites, Asians, and Hispanics in the NBA? Is Charlie Rangel demanding that Congress investigate? Will the Lakers someday have a five-foot-six Japanese center? Don't hold your breath.

What I'm driving at is this: We should *always* look for the best players for the team, whether it's in sports or medicine or fire fighting or law enforcement or academia or anything else. Enough of this affirmative-action crap. Make the rules fair for everybody and the best people will achieve.

Does saying that make me a racist? To some unhealthy individuals, yes.

Do I care? No, because nobody has found a way to shut me up when I'm right. On and off, I've been called racist for more than thirty years. I realize that if you don't march in lockstep and spout the party line, you have to learn to live with it. I remember one time in the early seventies I was doing my show in New York, and I was inveighing against illegitimacy. I remember saying, "What we have to do is stop encouraging women on welfare from having more babies that we have to pay for."

A woman called in, furious, and said, "Why'd you make that remark about black women?" And I said, "I never mentioned black or white."

"Yes, you did!" she insisted.

Just out of curiosity, we played the tape back. And race we never mentioned. But in *her* mind, it was a redundancy to say "black welfare mothers." If a white person said "welfare mothers," it was understood that he meant *black*. But that's not true. There are welfare mothers of every race. Here we are, in the nineties, with white illegitimacy growing by leaps and bounds.

Am I allowed to say that? Or am I being a racist *again*?

# America's Most
# Influential Bigots

—— ◆ ——

I THINK WE CAN ALL AGREE THAT THE MORE SOPHISTICATED AND MA-
ture any group becomes, the less its members will march
in lockstep. The smarter they are, the more divergent their
opinions. It just works out that way—an intelligent person is
confident enough to come to his or her own conclusions
without being told what to think.

So why is it that white liberals refuse to allow blacks to
enjoy freedom of thought?

These good, decent, tolerant liberal whites would never
*dream* of criticizing a white person for not spouting the official "white" party line. They wouldn't *think* of marginalizing
or ignoring a male for not holding the "male" point of view.
They couldn't *imagine* claiming that all Jews or Catholics or
Episcopalians agree on everything.

For some reason, though, they can't accept it when a black
person says something other than what they believe he or
she ought to say. These great white liberals and humanitar-
ians think they know best what blacks should believe—and
they have decided that all blacks must parrot the opinions
of Jesse Jackson, Al Sharpton, the NAACP, etcetera. Not coin-
cidentally, the same views held by . . . the great white fathers
of liberalism.

Think for a moment of how ridiculous it is to want all

members of any group to believe one thing only. Now think
of how condescending and belittling—how, well, *racist*—it
is to tell members of a group what, for their own good, they
*ought* to believe.

There was a time when blacks benefited from speaking with
one voice of solidarity and determination. But that time—before
the voting and other laws were changed to allow everyone full
participation in America—has passed. Since then, black opinion
has become so free and varied that there's now even a growing
army of genuine black intellectuals who hold nonliberal views.
Their names are legend on my show—Thomas Sowell, Joseph
Perkins, Walter Williams, Shelby Steele, Emanuel McLittle, just
to name a few. They disagree with liberalism's main points of
faith, such as affirmative action, welfare rights, and the glorifi-
cation and perpetuation of victimhood.

But the white liberal establishment refuses to see these
brave thinkers as anything but a small, unrepresentative
cadre of oddballs and contrarians. Time and time again,
that's how they are portrayed by our arrogant opinion-
molders of the left. If you're black and conservative, you are
by their definition the holder of a fringe view. Even worse—
your motive for holding such opinions is suspect.

I first noticed this when Nixon began his war on crime.
For some reason, it was assumed that only white conservatives wanted tough treatment for criminals. To what passes
for the liberal mind, "white conservative" equals "racist."
Therefore, blacks were expected to be in knee-jerk opposition
to it. The fact is that violent crimes—muggings, murders, bur-
glaries, rapes—are committed against blacks at a much higher
rate than against whites. Did the liberals think blacks didn't
mind getting hit over the head and robbed? Did they think
that blacks enjoyed seeing their streets littered with empty
crack vials? Or did the liberals simply believe that blacks
automatically root for criminals?

Today, liberals believe that all blacks should be in favor
of welfare and affirmative action. Do they think that no
blacks hold jobs or that they just love paying sky-high taxes
to support a bunch of moochers and their illegitimate offspring? Do they believe blacks welcome the suspicion that
all their gains are thanks to the white man's efforts to tilt the

playing field in their favor? Judging by how the media cover these issues, I guess they do!

I am no fan of Robin Quivers, Howard Stern's sidekick. But not long ago I saw her on the *Tonight* show, where she appeared with Linda Ronstadt. And out of nowhere, in a totally inappropriate and impolite way, Ronstadt laced into Quivers for not spouting the liberal party line whenever Stern starts bad-mouthing criminals and such. If I had a gun, I would have plugged my own TV—imagine the nerve of that nitwit telling Quivers that because she is black she must say what Ronstadt wants her to say. That's a liberal's idea of freedom—freedom to agree with liberals.

Here's another example of white liberal racism at work. Years ago, when I was on WMCA, I interviewed Myrtle Whitmore, a black woman from Brooklyn, who at that time was the president of the Crown Heights Civic and Taxpayers Association. As we talked, I found that she and I had many identical core beliefs and values. She was articulate and bright and charming, so much so that when I was planning a week's vacation, I suggested that she be hired to fill in for me.

Eventually, Peter Straus, the owner of the station, agreed, and she did so not once but twice, and admirably. Then, on a third occasion, when I recommended her again for the job, Straus suddenly was reluctant. She wasn't really representative of the black community, he had decided. She was too conservative.

Who did he suggest *should* take over the show during my vacation? Well, he wanted to hire the famed conservative Bobby Seale—the Black Panther thug who earned his fifteen minutes of fame in 1968, when he had to be bound and gagged during the trial of the Chicago Eight.

*That's* who Straus thought deserved to be called a representative of the black community—someone who wanted to burn the country down, someone who took up arms against the police and white America at large. Only *he,* Straus believed, could speak for all black Americans. Myrtle didn't satisfy Straus's idea of what a black person should be, because she loves her country and wants to make it work.

The most damning thing you can do to a black person is to label him what we used to call an Uncle Tom. Well, what *is* an Uncle Tom? Is an Uncle Tom someone who says, "Yes, boss, yessir," and then shuffles into the kitchen? That *used* to be true. Today, an Uncle Tom is a black who says that he doesn't need welfare or affirmative action or busing in order to enjoy life to the fullest and achieve what he or she deserves. I have heard whites privately refer to these people as "Oreos"—black on the outside and white on the inside. Imagine the colossal nerve of saying that a black person who doesn't hold certain views isn't *really* black at all. The white liberals even demand the power to decide who is black and who isn't. What nauseating hubris.

Calling someone an Oreo or a Tom or a traitor to his race is a way of labeling him into silence and infamy and nonexistence. Why do the good, tolerant liberal whites do this? For the same unhealthy psychological reason they do most things—guilt. They felt guilty enough to turn the world upside down looking for cosmetic ways to make up for the unfair treatment blacks used to receive. And then some blacks had the nerve to say they didn't need the patronizing white liberal "Great Society" treatment. That struck panic and fear into the liberal heart. And so the "ingrates" had to be punished.

That's the white liberal system of exterminating opposition. They control the labels. So they *mis*label all who talk back. If a white disagrees with them, he's a racist. If a black disagrees, he can't—*can't*—truly be black. It's a no-win situation, and it makes me sick.

The true beliefs of these liberals have been revealed lately by the widespread acceptance of a particularly nasty slur. It's been around for a while, but now you can find it in newspapers, magazines, TV shows, and everywhere else. The fact that these elitist snobs feel so comfortable using it tells me that ending bigotry is not truly their aim.

What's the term? "White trash." You'll hear the most politically correct phonies use it all the time. Never "black trash" or "yellow trash" or "brown trash"—only *white.* They have no compunctions about using a term that denigrates an entire group, in this case whites who don't have much education or earn much money and don't want to grow up to be paragons of virtue like Teddy Kennedy or Gloria Steinem. That makes them "trash"—disposable human beings—to the liberals. What a bunch of classist hypocrites.

# Why I Stopped Using the C-Word on the Air

——— ◆ ———

BELIEVE IT OR NOT, THERE ARE PEOPLE OUT THERE WHO WANT TO shut me up.

My enemies want to shut me up, which is understandable. But there have also been times when my friends—my teammates, my colleagues, my bosses—have wanted to shut me up, too. At times like those, I am reminded of what a lonely business speaking your mind for a living can be. In the end, no matter how high your ratings are or how much revenue you're bringing in, you're out there out your own.

You've all heard of the seven words you can't say on radio, the profanities and obscenities that, if uttered, may cost you your FCC license to broadcast. Well, I'm here to tell you that the list doesn't end at number seven. Not if you're Bob Grant, it doesn't.

In 1973 I was doing a show for WMCA in New York, and one day there was a news story about the inspection of beef. The story involved a United States congressman with whom I had once jousted. I joust with everybody sooner or later, of course, and it's rarely personal. I had never even met this man, and I barely remembered that our paths had ever crossed, even verbally.

Anyway, on this occasion I was in total agreement with the congressman's position on the beef inspections. So I asked my producer, Steve Grossman, to call the man—U.S. Representative Benjamin Rosenthal, of the Seventh Congressional District of New York, my own district back when I lived in Queens. I just wanted to discuss the controversy with him on the air.

A few minutes later Steve comes in and says that when he got Rosenthal on the phone, the congressman asked him, "Is this the guy I don't like?" So Steve said, "What do you mean?" Rosenthal replied, "Well, is this the guy who's on the air at such and such a time?" Steve said, "Yeah . . ." And Rosenthal said, "Well, I won't come on with him. I don't *want* to come on with him. Last time I was on with him, he gave me a pretty hard time."

End of conversation. Oh, well. Some people are just not built to handle public life.

About half an hour later I'm taking phone calls on different subjects, and somebody calls to complain about us allowing Soviet ships to dock in New York.

The caller said, "Bob, you oughta run for Congress." And I said, "Maybe I will, because as long as we have cowards like Ben Rosenthal running this country, we're not going to get anywhere." Now, the issue we were discussing had nothing to do with Rosenthal. But I wanted to have some fun—I was annoyed and wanted to needle him back for refusing to talk to me.

Well, lo and behold, Ben Rosenthal came out of hiding—he sued the station. Not for libel or slander, but because, according to the FCC rules in those days, a person, if attacked on a controversial issue, was to be notified. I knew the rule as well as Rosenthal did, but I had *already* called him once and he wouldn't even get on the phone with me.

In the first round he won the case, and the station was fined $10,000 for not notifying him. We appealed and the station won. In fact, Benno Schmidt, who was then of Yale Law School, acted as a friend of the court, and he took the side of WMCA.

And freedom of speech was thus defended and preserved, right? Don't be naive. The whole incident so traumatized WMCA's fainthearted owner, Peter Straus, that he took the extraordinary and perhaps unprecedented step of forbidding me to use the word "coward." Never again call anyone a coward, he ordered me.

This, may I remind you, was in 1974, a year when a great many forbidden words went public in movies, plays, books, and ordinary human discourse. In that year, I was forbidden to use the word "coward."

Could I allow such an idiotic, feckless restriction to silence me? Well, two years later, a man named Abe Beame was mayor of New York. And in the course of the show one day, a caller wanted to know why Mayor Beame hadn't spoken out against some black hooligans who were attacking people in Central Park. I said, "Well, sir, it's either that he's unaware of the situation or he's aware but he's too cowardly to take any action, or maybe both."

Did the wrath of Abe Beame then come crashing down upon my head? No—station owner Straus saved him the trouble. I was promptly suspended without pay for two days for having called Beame a coward. Correction: I didn't actually call him a coward. I suggested that maybe he was cowardly.

Straus suspended me long-distance, because he was in Washington that day. His wife, Ellen, was involved in running the station, too, so I went to her office to protest.

And here's what she said: "Well, why couldn't you have called him a scaredy-cat?"

I'm not making this up! Those were her exact words. I told her, "Ellen, it means the same thing!" But she repeated that I might not be in hot water had I used the word "scaredy-cat." She'd rather have had a talk-show host who sounded like a five-year-old than someone who tells it like it is. I quit that station on the air not long after, one of the happiest days of my professional life.

That was my misadventure with my very own c-word. It's not the only time this kind of nonsense has intruded on my rights. Once, in fact, I was prohibited by station management from using the z-word.

The z-word?

Many years ago, the opera singer Maria Callas was in the city of Chicago, and she was trying to make a point about how the crowds were acting outside the opera house. She said they were behaving like a bunch of wild Zulus, a turn of phrase I rather liked.

Not long after, while on the air in Los Angeles, I used the same word to describe a mob of white anti–Vietnam War protesters. If you look at the film of the incident I was describing, it was outside of Century Plaza Hotel. Lyndon Baines Johnson had to be sneaked in a back door because the crowd was so unruly.

Next thing you know the brass at Metromedia, which was the company that owned KLAC, my station then, held a meeting on the use of the word "Zulu" by Bob Grant. And I was asked by some official who'd come in from New York why I had chosen the word "Zulu."

I said, "Sir, I don't know specifically why I said 'Zulu' in the heat of the discussion—it just popped into my mind. But what's so terrible about what I said?"

He said, "Use of that kind of language could cost us our license."

Amazing. Someone at that meeting had said, "Well, what if Mr. Grant had called them a bunch of wild Indians?" And this guy replied, "Well, that would have been all right." That was in 1967 or 1968—just shows you how times have changed. Today they wouldn't let me call anybody a Zulu *or* a wild Indian.

Of course, I've gotten lots of grief for using the s-word.

Not *that* s-word. I had referred to the people who were screaming and hollering about the Rodney King case, burning down Los Angeles, as "savages." A caller mentioned the fact that there were people assembled in an African Methodist Episcopal church in Los Angeles delivering screeching tirades against the police and the white power structure—the usual suspects. And I said, "Well, I don't care if they're screaming in a church or rioting in the street—they're savages."

In this case, management didn't forbid me from using the word. But there are a lot of race-baiters out there who monitor my every word, and they pounced when I used this one. I tried to explain that "savage" describes a type of behavior, but *they* have decided that it's a synonym for "black." Just as they think "welfare recipient" and "black" are synonymous;

"illegitimate mother" and "black" are synonymous; "criminal" and "black" are synonymous. *I* don't think they're synonymous at all, and to suggest that they are is a terrible insult to all the blacks who get married, work hard for their money, and stay out of trouble with the law. But some jokers have so distorted everything that comes out of my mouth that it's almost impossible to have a meaningful discussion of these critical issues. Which is exactly how they like it.

There was another s-word I loved using, until management pressured me into dropping it from my vocabulary.

It was a good word, too. Sometimes I just get so furious at somebody, so outraged, that only the word "scumbag" will do. "Oh, shut up, you scumbag!" Has a nice ring, doesn't it?

Well, you'll never hear me utter that word on the air again. Even though they use it on *NYPD Blue,* which is also on ABC. Even though lots of other radio shows feel free to toss "scumbag" around the airwaves.

# Some Final Words
# About David Clark

———— ◆ ————

HE IS DEAD NOW, WHICH MAY BRING HIS PERSECUTORS SOME SATIS
faction, for it was only his silence they wanted. But because
he reached his destiny through his connection with me, I
must tell what he cannot.

I first heard of David Clark on January 30, 1992. He called
the show and identified himself only as David of Asbury
Park. He was a teacher, he said, who was troubled by something going on at his high school.

The trouble, to his mind, was symbolized by banners that
had gone up all over the place—"Black History Month: 200
Years in America, 2,000 Years in Africa," they proclaimed.

David said that for the observance, he had assigned to his
English classes some poems by Langston Hughes and the
works of a few other black authors. The principal, he said,
informed him that he wasn't doing enough and should include even more readings for the occasion.

At that point, David said, he balked. "Look," he told the
principal, "I teach English, not history. And you're calling
it Black *History* Month." In truth, David continued, he had
problems with the entire concept of a month devoted to just
one segment of his students.

And then he went further and spoke an opinion that struck
even me as a little intemperate, though understandable. For-

86

tunately, we live in a country where every viewpoint may be expressed.

Here's what David said: "Black History Month is a joke. In two hundred years we went to the moon. After two thousand years they're still urinating in their drinking and bathing water."

Strong words. Without a doubt, offensive to some. But still, exactly the kind of expression we must protect. His opinions were not nearly as inflammatory as some of the views put forth by Leonard Jeffries, the anti-Semitic, anti-white genius of the New York City university system.

I asked David where he taught, expecting him to decline to answer, but he didn't—he freely stated that he worked at Neptune High School, in central New Jersey, and had been a teacher for twenty years.

I don't know for sure what happened next. Somehow, a tape and transcript of Clark's comments fell into the hands of Neptune's principal and the New Jersey NAACP.

Immediately, David was suspended without pay from his job. When I heard, I called him and offered commiseration and the chance to appear on my show to tell what had happened. He thanked me but said his lawyer had advised him to lie low and hope for reinstatement soon.

I told my audience what had befallen Clark, how he had been made to suffer for expressing an unpopular, strong opinion. To my way of thinking, he should have been allowed to say what he said even in a classroom. In America, we allow all sides to be heard and trust ourselves to listen and then do what's right.

But he didn't say it in class or even on school time. He said it as David Clark, citizen of America.

For the next two and a half years, David sought to regain what had been stolen from him. The school district would not budge on its dismissal of the teacher who dared to speak his mind. But neither would David budge.

Finally, in 1994, a judge forced Neptune Union High School to reinstate David Clark as a teacher.

That was just after he and I first met, face to face. I was attending a political fund-raiser in Montclair, New Jersey, when the hostess came up to me in the company of a man and said, "Bob, do you know David Clark?"

"Well," I said, "David, how *are* you?" I knew the answer just by looking at him" Not well. At the age of forty-six, he was dying of pancreatic cancer.

He finally got his job back, so justice had been done, in a way. But not in a way that did David any good. The cancer finally killed him in February of 1995. He never stepped back inside a classroom.

Now, of course, people die from cancer every day. But David had not been ill prior to his dismissal. I firmly believe that the persecution of David Clark was in part what brought on the cancer. I know for sure that the mind affects the body. You need an extremely strong constitution to withstand the withering attacks the Thought Police can dish out today.

I know that better than most. But I am a paid pariah, fully aware that if I state my honest opinions, I am going to be vilified. There are some who actually go out of their way to become pariahs. Just after the Oklahoma City bombing last year, G. Gordon Liddy showed that he is one of those. He aired his outrageous opinion that citizens may feel free to shoot government agents, knowing exactly what it would do for his fledgling radio career.

But what about David Clark? What happens to the ordinary citizen who expresses an unpopular thought? He soon learns that he has nothing to gain from speaking his mind. And much to lose.

# Ten Conservatives We Can Live Without

———— ◆ ————

1. *George Bush*—When he ran on Reagan's coattails, he donned the cloak of a conservative. When he ran against Dukakis, he did likewise. But he has never been a *true* conservative. He was born a rich WASP and decided that he'd serve government, because that's what they do, out of their sense of noblesse oblige. But he revealed his lack of principles when he signed the tax increase of 1990 and when he pushed for the Americans With Disabilities Act and the affirmative action guidelines. He's an elitist Ivy League Republican—not a conservative at all. And he cost us the White House.

2. *Bill Bennett*—A smart man with a keen mind and the manners of a bull in a china shop. He had absolutely no business going to California and attempting to undermine Pete Wilson and the effort to pass Proposition 187. He hurt the valid conservative cause of limiting immigration, and he brought aid and comfort to those twin hazards, Dianne Feinstein and Kathleen Brown. He's an amateur politician trying to pretend he's a real one.

3. *Jack Kemp*—He, too, went to California and openly opposed Proposition 187. So I automatically dislike him. Plus, I've met him several times over the past two decades, and we've shared many a dais, but each time he sees me he sticks

out his big hand and introduces himself as though we've never met.

4. *Pat Robertson*—I resent his efforts to take the Republican party hostage and use it to further his wacko ideas and his own personal religious agenda. I don't agree with the Council on Foreign Relations or the Trilateral Commission any more than he does, but unlike Pat, I don't believe they're agents of the Antichrist.

5. *Christine Whitman*—Another Republican who's not a conservative. No sooner did she get elected than she began going out of her way to attack Pat Buchanan and other right-wingers. She's devoid of any clear philosophical underpinning, and so she tries to appease the left-leaning fringe of the Republican party. She's George Bush in a skirt.

6. *Spiro T. Agnew*—For old times' sake. Because he could deliver Bill Safire's brilliant words so well, Agnew became the darling of the nation's conservatives during Nixon's first term. As the flames of Watergate began consuming Nixon, all our hopes flew to Agnew, but he broke our hearts when, in 1973, he admitted that he was just another crooked, self-serving Maryland pol. Because he was more charismatic than Nixon, he damaged conservatism even more than his boss did.

7. *Ollie North*—I supported the Contra cause, and at the time he became a controversial figure, I supported North's actions in the Iran-Contra affair. But I no longer believe that he did the Contras *or* his boss, Ronald Reagan, any favors. North broke the law, and no good can come of that, regardless of the rightness of the cause. I also have a problem with people using their notoriety to launch careers in talk radio, as North did.

8. *George Will*—A brilliant guy who has articulated conservative beliefs also almost as well as William F. Buckley, the master. But Will keeps repeating the same inane mantra—that we Americans are actually *undertaxed*. Doesn't he realize that his words encourage politicians to do the wrong thing? (Not that they need much encouragement.) If he finds himself with too much money after the tax man takes his bite, let George Will fund a few social programs out of his own pocket. But leave our dough alone.

9. *G. Gordon Liddy*—He gives me credit for his presence in talk radio today, but I still include him here. He is a gentleman when you meet him, but he is also the man who tells his listeners that if ATF agents enter their homes without warrants, it's okay to open fire on them. Under *no* circumstances is it okay to shoot a law officer, and Liddy knows that.

10. *Rush Limbaugh*—I should say he's a conservative whom *I* can live without. Because without him on the scene, I like to think, then *I* would be the most popular conservative talk-radio personality in America. Why couldn't he have been born a liberal?

# Showbiz Days

◆

I DON'T LIKE TO ADMIT THIS, BUT SINCE NOBODY READS BOOKS ANY-more, I feel safe in revealing that I never intended to go into broadcasting. Not only that, had I followed my true dream, I believe, I would be a happier, more fulfilled man today.

As a junior at Steinmetz High School back in Chicago, I somehow ended up in a drama class. The teacher was Ruby Yetter, a lovely woman who had a terribly mottled complexion, so much so that we callous lads named her after the Chester Gould cartoon character "Pruneface."

Anyway, almost from the first day of class she began telling me that I should seriously consider a life in the theater. To prove her sincerity, she recommended that I be auditioned for the Central Radio Workshop of the Chicago Public Schools. To be selected to participate was a great honor, because only a handful of students could take part.

After auditioning, I was accepted, which meant that once every two weeks I was excused from class to work at the school system's FM station. It's now a giant operation, WBEZ, but back then people barely knew what FM *was*. My father had to go out and buy a new radio, a big monstrosity, just to be able to hear me on the air.

We would do what were called learning dramas, plays

such as *Rivers of America* and others whose titles I no longer recall.

I do remember that on one of my first days there, the station's director, Robert R. Miller, said, "Gigante, you'll make a million in this business." This in the days when very few people could even dream of amassing such a sum. I mean, the average professional baseball player was probably making $8,000 a year back then. But when Mr. Miller said that, he spoke with such authority that I believed him. He made it sound as though radio would be my destiny.

But not the kind of radio I do now. We performed plays on the air. In fact, I then became very active in the theater scene at school. The play I remember best was *Ghost of the Air,* which was about a murder that had been committed in a radio studio. I played Jasper Holmes, the detective who cracked the case.

At the University of Illinois I also auditioned for the school radio station and was accepted. The school's drama program, the Illini Theater, was casting for its annual play, and its director, the distinguished professor Charles Schattuck, was holding auditions for parts in *The Duchess of Malfi,* by Shakespeare's contemporary, John Webster.

I was the new guy, and barely aware of the tryouts, but a friend encouraged me to audition, so I did. A few days later he called and said, "You son of a gun, you got the part of the Duke of Calabria!" It was one of the three leads. It was a huge part, all in Elizabethan verse. I had to wear tights, a goatee, and all the rest of the regalia. I loved it.

Also while in college I played the part of Jacob, the grandfather, in *Awake and Sing* at the Jewish People's Institute, which was very prominent then. Afterward, people were coming backstage, saying, "No, no—the way you played that part, you must be Jewish." So I was pretty good, I guess.

Not long after that, I got my first job in broadcasting, purely by accident. I answered a phone call for my roommate, who wanted to be in radio. The caller was a radio program director trying to fill a slot, and he liked the sound of my voice and offered the job to me, and I took it.

But I kept acting, as a hobby. Years later, in Los Angeles, I joined Actors' Equity and was in a couple of plays. I was the Ragpicker in *The Madwoman of Chaillot,* for instance. Got some good reviews, too. As a matter of fact, I never got anything but good reviews in any plays I did.

I actually returned to broadcast acting, in a way. In the late fifties, I worked on something called *The Gold Coast Show,* a radio program that featured comedy skits. As a result of that, I did another show, with a partner, that was almost like *Saturday Night Live* on radio. It was way ahead of its time. My partner and I wrote the show and performed it. We did spoofs. We did takeoffs. We did hoaxes, some that were so convincing, CBS News asked us to continually remind the listeners. Once we broke in with a news bulletin announcing that Fidel Castro's beard had accidently been shaved off. Another time, we turned the broadcast over to a "live transmission" from the floor of the United Nations General Assembly, where "Adlai Stevenson" (me, doing a very good impression) flipped out and began screaming at the Soviet ambassador.

But not long after that, I fell into talk radio, and have been here pretty much ever since.

I still regret that I didn't become a professional actor. I might not have been as successful financially, but I think it would have been more rewarding personally. Nobody believes me when I say this, but I don't like doing a call-in talk-radio show. I honestly feel that I've never fulfilled my real potential. I know that may sound egotistical and self-serving, but it's true.

I think I didn't want to pay the price for devoting my life to the theater. I knew lots of good actors and actresses who starved. Back in Chicago I knew an actor who was part of a local theater group. He visited me at my radio job one day and said, "Hey, Bob, do you think you could get me some work here as an announcer? I have a pretty good voice." And he did, too. But he wasn't making ends meet on stage. A few years later, he went to Hollywood, left serious acting, and became a comedian—a famous one, too—by the name of Shelley Berman. But as talented as he was, he couldn't make it on acting, either.

A life in the theater is an insecure living. It's a very demanding, very chancy existence. When my father heard a teacher say that I had a future in acting, he was a little worried. "I thought you wanted to go to law school," he said to me. "Lawyers are the greatest actors of all. And you need something to fall back on." And I kept hearing that phrase, "to fall back on," and I guess it implies that you'll fail at what you really want to do. So there was that. And I didn't expect to be making good money in radio, but before long I was. I still could have chosen the stage, I guess, but being basically lazy, I took the lazy way out.

# The Sporting Life

$$\blacklozenge$$

I REALIZE NOW THAT I AM SO GOOD AT MY JOB BECAUSE I AM A veritable factory of opinions. I form opinions the way other people exhale. There's almost no subject on which I don't have a view that I can argue convincingly from a sound philosophical basis.

In fact, the first opinions I ever uttered over the airwaves were on a subject that holds almost no interest at all for me—sports.

Believe it or not, I was the sports director of KABC back in Los Angeles a thousand years ago. I would do a couple of sports reports during the day, but the best part of my job was the commentaries. The station wanted a Howard Cosell–type presence, and I was it. I was very opinionated and contentious, which got the listeners' attention. For example, I did an editorial on why Dodger Stadium had so few water fountains, and I ventured a guess that it had something to do with owner Walter O'Malley's wish to sell lots of beer and soft drinks to the fans. Every station today has loudmouth sports announcers, but back then it was a novelty.

But my first venture into sports radio was a disaster that seemed, at the time, like a career ender. In 1954, I was working for CBS in Chicago, and back then they did a nationwide round-robin of college football games. The show was anchored by Red Barber in New York, and he would switch around from game to game throughout the country. He'd say, "All right—let's see now. The battle for the Little Brown Jug is just getting underway in Ann Arbor, Michigan, so let's swing out to Joe Blow in Ann Arbor, Michigan. Joe?"

And the announcer would say, "Thank you, Red. Hello, fans everywhere. The ball is on the fifteen yard line, in possession of Minnesota. It's first and ten, McNamara's at quarterback, *blah blah blah . . .*" And for two minutes his play-by-play would go out over the network.

Now, how did a nonfan like me end up pulling this duty? Only because the regular announcer's wife was having a baby and the usual stand-in was sick. When the program director of WBBM asked the announcers if any of us had play-by-play experience, I lied and said I had covered high school football. Why did I do it? Just to see if I could handle the job.

Anyway, this was on a Friday, so I rushed to the airport and got to Ann Arbor. I was told I'd have a veteran "spotter" to help me out. Now, even the most seasoned play-by-play man needs a good spotter. It's your job to watch the action and call it, and it's his job to tell you exactly which player has the ball or makes the tackle or whatever. The stadium in Ann Arbor is vast. It seats more than one hundred thousand people, and it is wide and sprawling. The broadcast booth is a *long* way from the field, and you can't announce, look through binoculars to see the players' numbers, *and* consult the player list all at the same time. That's why a spotter is vital.

But when I arrived at the booth, I was told the spotter was out sick, too. They assured me that his replacement would do just fine. A little later, he came in—an average-looking college kid in white bucks, blue blazer, and crewcut. He didn't exactly inspire confidence, but the game was about to start.

Next thing I know, there's Red Barber's voice coming through my headphones. It just happened to be a very exciting moment in the game. Michigan had the ball on Minnesota's fifteen-yard line. Red turned it over to me, and I said, "All right, the ball is snapped, and it's handed off to . . ." And then I looked to the spotter for the runner's name.

And the spotter gives me a huge shrug and mouths the words "I don't know!"

So I say, "The backfield man is running with it, and he is brought down at the..." And again I look to the spotter. Who *again* shrugs as he struggles with the binoculars.

"... by Minnesota's ..."

Another shrug. Another pleading look accompanied by the words "I don't know!"

He wasn't the only one panicking. I wanted to die right then and there—right after I killed this kid. But it got worse. We were supposed to stay on for no more than two minutes, but nobody remembered to start the stopwatch, so I had no idea where I was, timewise. Not only was my broadcast an inept mess, but I had gone way over my time.

Mercifully, I made it to the end of the spot. I got a call from the network saying that Red Barber was furious with me. So I got chewed out royally for staying on too long.

Barber then had the courage to come back to me a little later in the game, but it was the same disaster: "All right—there's a high, end-over-end kick, coming down on the ..." And the spotter still couldn't manage to tell me where the ball was. A catastrophe.

I still don't know how I got through that day. When I got back to Chicago, one of my coworkers offered to play for me a tape of my broadcast. I begged off.

"You can't take it, huh?" he said.

I said, "Well, you tell me. Was it as bad as I think?"

He said, "You don't have a thing to worry about!"

"I *don't?*" I said.

"Nope—they'll never ask you to do *that* again!"

And they never did, either. But I found something to be proud of in that nightmare. I lived through it, and stayed in radio anyway.

# III

# Whose Government Is This, Anyway?

———— ◆ ————

*The career politicians and bureaucrats, along with the pundits of the left, are currently wailing and keening over what they depict as dangerous "antigovernment" sentiment at loose in the land, but they're way off base. Most people believe strongly in our form of government. We just don't like how it has been perverted and contorted out of shape over the past few decades.*

*Our dissatisfaction has two main, related causes.*

*First, government does too many things we don't want it to do. In fact, the general drift of government activism has been to do things that help small minorities and special interests at the expense of the majority.*

*Second, every time the government does anything, it ends up costing us too much money. The costs nearly always outweigh the benefits.*

*In other words, the people who pay for government are the people whom government seems least interested in serving. You could even say that we pay government to do things that damage us. But we're not angry at government—just at some of the bozos who run it.*

# Injustice for All

———— ◆ ————

Dɪᴅ ʏᴏᴜ ʙᴇɴᴇꜰɪᴛ ꜰʀᴏᴍ ᴛʜᴇ ɪɴꜱᴛɪᴛᴜᴛɪᴏɴ ᴏꜰ ꜱʟᴀᴠᴇʀʏ? Lᴜᴄᴋʏ ʏᴏᴜ
if you did, because that would mean your ancestors owned
big spreads of farmland and other choice real estate, and
chances are that dough is still in your family.

I sure as hell didn't benefit from slavery. From the sixteenth to the nineteenth centuries, my ancestors were a
bunch of goombahs working like mules on farms in southern
Italy. They weren't slaves, but their day-to-day lives were no
different from those of captive Africans tilling the red soil of
Georgia. Like most of the planet's population in that age, my
ancestors, too, had no choice but to work like beasts of burden or starve to death. In fact, after Booker T. Washington
visited southern Italy in the nineteenth century, he reported
that the peasants there had it worse even than the slaves in
the American South.

There—now don't you feel sorry for me? Isn't there something you want to give me to salve your guilty conscience?
Some of that extra money you have lying around in the bank
or a better job than I really deserve or a break on my college
boards or my tuition to Harvard?

Oh, no? Bigot.

What's that you say? Didn't *I* benefit from the unequal
laws that governed postslavery racial relations here? From

Jim Crow and other antiblack discrimination in hiring, housing, and so on?

Well, sure, I did. All white Americans did. I never *asked* to be treated a certain way just because I was white. But I was given preferential treatment compared with what blacks got. And that was wrong, and un-American, too. If we're going to boast that we're the land of the fair shake, we have to live up to that.

Once reasonable Americans realized how unfair the laws were, we changed them. The playing field was made flat. It became illegal to give different opportunities to people based on their race, which is how it should be.

But the playing field didn't stay flat for long. Soon, it began to tilt in the other direction. Laws were passed and rules and quotas and goals and guidelines were adopted that brought about the ugly spectacle of more discrimination—this time, *reverse* discrimination.

No wonder people started to wonder, "Was a flat playing field what these activists *really* wanted all along?"

Or were they saying, "Preferential treatment, unjust advantages, special considerations, and an inside edge are all bad if they favor you—but wonderful if they favor *us*"?

I believe that's *exactly* what they're saying. It's a sad truth about the lower aspect of human nature: though people love to wrap themselves in the cloak of righteousness, we really aren't very principled deep inside. We rail against unfairness when it works against *us*. We hate privilege when somebody else has it and we don't. Or, in the good liberal way, we're in favor of special advantages for others—only *if* we're sure we won't have to sacrifice anything or suffer as a result.

The humane and benevolent Illinois State University, for example, was all for discrimination when it created a no-whites-allowed course—to train people to become janitors. What do you think the response would have been if, instead, Harvard's Medical School or the Wharton School of Business had decided to admit minorities only? Even your most sanctimonious liberal philosopher, if faced with a situation that endangered *his* goodies, would suddenly become as base and grasping and selfish as anyone else.

There's a guy I know. He went to the same Ivy League

school his father attended and graduated with a valuable degree and an impressive Rolodex of classmates and fellow alumni to call on when the need arises. He inherited enough money to ensure a nice unearned income on top of the big bucks he's pulling down in his chosen profession. He and his family live in a lovely upper-middle-class palace, surrounded by other people of similar mannerly, agreeable background and values. He has cars and an office and a place in the country to complement the splendor of everything else he possesses. He has the good taste to frequent fancy restaurants where he is instantly recognized, fawned over, adored, and coddled to his heart's content.

Now, here's what I want to know: When is the government going to do something about all *his* unearned, unfair privileges? When is this guy going to be forced by law to have lunch at his private club with worthy minorities who otherwise couldn't get inside the place (except maybe as busboys)? When is he going to have to share his favorite table with someone who maybe can't afford to be a regular at the restaurant but is otherwise a very fine person? When will our legislators make this guy invite a disadvantaged person along on his annual ski trip to Gstaad? When will he be ordered to open his Rolodex to every deserving man and woman with no Rolodex of their own?

Keep waiting. Bring your lunch. It'll be a while.

Affirmative action is the single most horrifying example of what happens when liberal "good" intentions are taken to their evil, destructive extreme. Supposedly, affirmative action was going to make life in America more just. It did this by legislating injustice.

How did it all start? With a good deed, naturally. The passage of the Civil Rights Act of 1964, which rightly outlawed racial discrimination, brought us true equality of opportunity in the eyes of the law. That, supposedly, was what all the civil rights activists and Freedom Riders had prayed for.

And things in America were finally just and right—and they stayed that way for about five minutes. Because then, some so-called leaders said, "Hold on—the new laws are meaningless unless they produce the results we desired."

We know now what a fatal mistake that was. Even the

Declaration of Independence said only that all men are *created* equal and endowed by their creator with certain unalienable rights, among those life, liberty, and the pursuit of happiness. Our Founding Fathers wanted to guarantee the right of all Americans to *pursue* happiness on an equal basis. They didn't try to legislate the *result* of that pursuit. The best a government can do, they reckoned, was to make sure everybody had an equal shot at what they wanted and then get out of the way. After that, people will achieve and acquire more or less what they deserve, what they want and are willing to work for.

But no, the liberal intellectual giants of the sixties and seventies said, that's not enough. We must enforce equality not only at the starting line of the race but at the finish line as well, and every step in between.

At first, they talked about "outreach" programs that would encourage minorities to take advantage of newly opened opportunities in the workplace, education, job-training, and so on. Nobody argued with that, because it sounded reasonable and fair. It even sounded okay to me.

But as time went on, it became clear that simply reaching out and encouraging weren't working. Or they weren't working fast enough, at any event. Blacks were still not a proportionately large enough part of middle-class American life. They still weren't getting into colleges or managerial jobs or onto the boards of publicly held companies, at the rate some people had wished they would.

Well, how do you solve that one? By creating policies that *force* minorities into jobs and school, of course. By passing laws that mandate hiring quotas and minority preference when it comes time to grant government contracts to businesses. LBJ himself, in a speech, called for "equality of result." In other words, his goal wasn't to secure equal rights for blacks. He didn't care whether they earned success or not; he just wanted them to *have* it. He wanted his guilty conscience eased the second he snapped his fingers. This thinking, aided by the Labor Department and the federal Equal Employment Opportunity Commission, then trickled down to state and local governments, private industry, and universities, to ensure that the unfairness was spread around evenly.

Do you know who first called it "affirmative action"? Nobody famous—a bureaucrat from the JFK-LBJ era—but it's worth a moment's notice. It is a lesson in how language is manipulated in order to make something bad sound like something good. For whom is this action "affirmative"? By definition, for the minority of the population. For its beneficiaries, it is truly *affirmative* to receive something unearned. But what does this action mean for the majority of Americans? Nothing affirmative about it if *you* were passed over for a job or a spot in a college freshman class, you'll agree. Its rightful name where you're concerned is "negative action." That's what we should have been calling it all along, because you can't give somebody something unless you take it away from somebody else. So why did its supporters decide against calling it "negative action"? Ask George Orwell.

Nobody can deny that affirmative action is by definition a bad thing. It helps some people based on their race or gender and hurts others for the same reason. Not exactly the color-blind society everyone was supposedly dreaming of.

But wait, its supporters say. True, it *does* create a certain amount of unfairness, but nothing like the injustice of the bad old days before the Civil Rights Act. And this injustice has a noble purpose—it helps people who need it.

Is that so?

Do you know whom affirmative action helps? So far it has helped white middle-class females more than any other group. They, much more than any racial minority, have used the unfair laws and discriminatory rules to ascend into high positions at work and school. Do *they* really need the help from government? No—they would have prospered anyway, thanks simply to their good middle-class origins and values. But if we're offering them advantages because they were born female, they won't turn them down. I wouldn't, either—just as during the bad old days of Jim Crow, white Americans took advantage of bigotry and discrimination.

Affirmative action has also helped *certain* blacks and Hispanics. But since almost one-fifth of American blacks haven't finished high school, relaxed college admissions policies aren't helping them one bit. According to the U.S. Census, twenty-three percent of black men in their twenties are either in jail, on probation, or on parole. Twenty-three percent of black teenage females are unwed mothers. Those unfortunates aren't benefiting from *The New York Times*'s minority hiring quotas either. Middle-class blacks and Latinos are the ones who benefit from these policies. Those who come from nice, comfortable homes, from smart, educated, achievement-oriented families. Do *they* really need the help from government? No, but they're glad to take it, too. Joseph Perkins, a black newspaper columnist whom I read avidly, writes that affirmative action "is little more than a placebo. It gives advantaged blacks—better educated, professional, middle class—a leg up on comparable whites. But it does nothing to improve the prospects of the high school dropouts."

Who *suffers* because of affirmative action? Well, the answer is clear—whites and Asians. *Certain* whites and Asians, I should say. Let's face it, if you have money and connections, you won't have to sacrifice no matter what the laws say. If your father went to Yale, you will, too. If your parents are both physicians, your chances of growing up to be a janitor are fairly slim.

But if you're white and your father was a welder and you wish to go to Yale, nobody will give you a break. In fact, affirmative action may cost you the place there you rightly earned. If your parents are Korean immigrants who own a grocery and you want to be a fireman, there's no quota to ensure you a job. You may actually be denied a job because of the color of your skin. If you're white or Asian and from the middle class, affirmative action will hurt you and discriminate against you. It will wrongly treat you as though you've had it easier than the son of a black lawyer or a Hispanic millionaire. You will be denied your chance to fairly pursue happiness by the illogic and insanity of affirmative action.

Was this what its proponents desired? I can't pretend to know why they believed that doing something wrong would turn out right. They're not helping ghetto blacks and Hispanics, but they don't really care. They just wanted to assuage their guilt by helping *some* less advantaged group, whether they needed help or not. They are hurting some whites on the basis of their race, but again, the high and mighty liberals don't care. No member of the ruling class wanted their kids to become fireman or attend no-name universities anyway. The liberals' top priority wasn't helping disadvantaged people. They just wanted to be sure the world bought their act as card-carrying benevolent, tolerant, loving, giving, great white fathers. They say they wanted to bring "diversity" to American life, but that's a load of crap. *They're* still surrounded and protected by their fellow rich white snobs. They just wanted to be able to pat each other on the back and say, "My, aren't we nice guys?" That's the true goal of affirmative action, and guess what? It worked like a charm.

The final victim of affirmative action is America itself. It suffers when its laws are unjust. It suffers when its citizens are denied rights because of the color of their skin or their gender. And it suffers in more practical ways, too. Undermining a system that rewards merit means that everything ends up dumber and worse and shabbier and more incompetent than it has to be. People who deserve jobs don't get them, while people who don't deserve them do. A smarter person is denied a promotion, while a dumber one gets it. A motivated student is turned down for university admission, while one who has shown less desire to learn gets in. What could all that possibly do except sabotage excellence?

The University of California recently decided to drop affirmative action from its admissions policy. Just before it took that admirable step, the university looked at what would happen if affirmative action no longer played a part in admissions. Of the freshmen admitted in 1994, 41.7 percent were Asian-American. But had there been no affirmative action, they would have constituted as much as 54.7 percent of the class. Whites made up 29.8 percent, but 37 percent would have been white had there been no reverse discrimination. So it's clear—a fair number of whites and Asians who deserved to get in were turned away. On the other side of the ledger, Hispanics made up 15.3 percent of the class. But without any special favors, they would have been no more than 6.3 percent. Blacks composed 6.4 percent of the freshmen; without affirmative action, the class would have been no more than 2 percent black.

What does that tell you? First, it says that blacks and Hispanics who truly deserved admission will never know whether it was their brains or their skin that got them in. That doesn't sound like much of a favor to me. Second, it says that there are a lot of whites and even more Asians who have been getting screwed by the University of California, a publicly funded entity. These are your tax dollars at work.

Finally, it says that the students who wished to excel at the University of California were held back because they were sharing classrooms and teachers with classmates who were less able to absorb an education. That means the education gotten there was inferior to what it could have been were it not for affirmative action. Inferior education equals an inferior future—for those kids, for California, and for America.

Affirmative action costs us money, too (what a surprise). Presidential candidate Steve Forbes, estimates that in duplication of services, added bureaucracy, and wasteful spending on contracts with minority-owned firms that were not the lowest bidders, affirmative action has cost this country more than $1 trillion.

The people responsible for this nightmare haven't asked for my solution yet, but I'll offer it anyway. I actually do have a model on which we can base our policies for racial fairness in hiring and school admissions.

Look to the National Basketball Association for wisdom in this realm. In the NBA, there are no quotas or guidelines or goals or laws regarding race. The owners hire the best players they can afford, and that's that. The NBA is so completely color-blind that nobody even notices if, for whatever reasons, one race is represented in greater numbers than another. How well you play the game is all that matters, end of story. That principle is so clearly fair and just that no one even suggests tampering with the excellence of the game by legislating something as immaterial as its racial makeup. To even recommend such a thing would bring great heaps of ridicule and disgust down upon your empty head.

And do you know what? Basketball today is better than

it's ever been. It's one of the few aspects of American life about which you can say such a thing. The players are bigger, stronger, and more talented than ever. They jump higher, shoot more accurately, and provide a greater spectacle than ever before in the history of the sport. And there's no obstacle in its path toward even greater glory. Could we have said the same if membership in the league were decided by anything but talent? If the team owners decided they would consciously reject the best players in favor of worse ones, would the game be as great?

No.

# Vanity,
# Thy Name Is LBJ

◆

I HAVE A CONFESSION TO MAKE: THE CONCEPT OF SOMEONE NEEDING a handout from the government in order to survive—in other words, *welfare*—is not something I have viewed only from a great distance.

I'm afraid I'm old enough to recall hearing about relatives who benefited from what was then known as "home relief." Welfare. I remember my mother telling me once that Uncle Lou was crying. "Why is he crying?" I wondered, fearful. "Because he had to go on relief," she said gravely.

So my own Uncle Lou needed government money. And, of course, the government can't give Uncle Lou anything without first taking it from somebody else. The taxpayers had to kick in $50 a month so Uncle Lou, Aunt Connie, and my cousin Corinne could get by. That was a shock to the family. We all felt bad for Uncle Lou, but we were also queasy about the fact that he was taking something for nothing. Certainly he felt worse than any of us. He felt ashamed.

Before long, Uncle Lou found a backbreaking job with a dairy, one that paid him the handsome sum of $40 a week. But when he received that first paycheck and went off welfare, he had a huge smile—a smile of relief, you could call it—on his face.

He wasn't the exception during the Depression. Lots of

people who wanted desperately to work ended up on the dole. They *all* died a little inside with every handout they took.

Back then, the government didn't do anything to ease such feelings of shame, either. Relief was considered to be a bad thing all around, by the givers and the takers. A *necessary* thing, sometimes, but not desirable. Going on welfare was thought of as a crisis, and though we all need help during crises, nobody wants to live that way for long.

How did we lose those healthy feelings of shame when it comes to welfare? Not just the takers, but the givers, too?

Greater philosophers than I have noted the overall loss of shame in the American character these days. But I believe that something also happened to the way we think about poverty. Now, you might reply, "Sure, Grant, it's easy for you to say," but this is true: There will always be poor people. Some will be poor for a short period, and either luck or determination will raise them out of poverty. Others will, for whatever reasons, stay poor. Not that it's easy to be poor. Even earning a little money, if you're ignorant or unskilled or dumb, is hard work.

You know, Jesus Christ Himself said, "The poor will always be with us." And people pretty much accepted that as true—until Lyndon Baines Johnson came along and said in a speech, "Before this generation of Americans is finished, poverty will not only retreat, it will be conquered."

Well, well—maybe LBJ looked in his heart and found wisdom and kindness beyond what Christ could manage.

LBJ decided that poverty was something the government could step in and *conquer,* like a military foe. He and his fellow do-good Democrats announced that they were going to shoulder the task of wiping out a condition that has existed since the dawn of mankind. Every living thing has always known that you must work in order to survive. If they could speak, every pigeon scratching for bread crumbs in the park would tell you that. Every lizard hunting for insects would concur wholeheartedly. Only the utopian socialistic Democratic party of the sixties would disagree.

Now, you could call trying to end poverty among civilized people a noble, ambitious goal. A worthy endeavor. But in

**111**

the end, it's proven to be a foolish undertaking. There's no poverty *germ*. Poverty isn't an enemy that can be defeated on the battlefield. It's simply part of the human condition.

Thirty years A.J. (after Johnson), has poverty been eliminated? Not that I've noticed. In fact, it's gotten worse. Once upon a time, poor Americans harbored the hope that someday, if they persisted, they'd be better off. Today that hope seems all but gone. Today, the American ideal of bettering yourself has completely bypassed large chunks of the population. Some immigrants still strive to improve their circumstances. For them, poverty will be but a temporary thing—a bittersweet memory—the way it is for the descendants of those who came to this country early in the century.

But for the others, poverty will be a permanent fact of life. There are people born today who will never even realize that there's a connection between work and survival. They'll certainly never feel a twinge of shame at having to live off the rest of us. Once poverty became something that could be "defeated," the poor were encouraged to see themselves as its *victims*—as blameless creatures deserving sympathy and relief, just like casualties of war or disease. As a result, the payments the government makes to the poor have expanded dramatically beyond what we once gave. We used to throw the needy a rope; now we've created an entire "safety net" of programs to coddle them from the womb to the tomb. And the handouts are now called, in bureaucratic jargon, "entitlements." That's exactly how the recipients see them—as what they're *entitled* to get. Nobody feels ashamed to take what they believe to be rightly theirs.

And still we're trying, naively, to end poverty, to the tune of $300 billion in payments a year. At a certain point, you could say, naivete becomes plain old stupidity. Because on the way to eradicating poverty, we're about to become poor ourselves. In fact, we're already there—almost $5 trillion in debt. In trying to end poverty for some Americans, we've impoverished America itself.

The Depression toughened up a lot of American people, I believe. But it didn't do much to improve anybody who was eager to take a handout. For it was also during the Depression that farm subsidies became widespread. And even though most people don't think of them as welfare, that's exactly what they are.

America's farmers needed help during the Depression, just like everybody else. But once those dark days ended, did the subsidies end, too? No—government programs are harder to kill than vampires. So here we are today, the largest agricultural exporter in the world. There are global markets that just wait and hope for American agricultural products. That, plus our own expanding population, guarantees the huge and growing demand for what we grow and raise. And, yet, we still have a farm subsidy program.

Are the farmers ashamed to take subsidies? Hardly. Every now and then you'll see a television news report showing farmers in Wisconsin or whatever openly dumping milk! They'll take dairy subsidies, and then drive up the price of their product by destroying it. Or you'll hear of a bumper crop in corn, soybeans, wheat, or whatever, and think that the farmers must be happy. But they're not! Because the more grain they produce, the lower the price per bushel.

And so the government comes along and says, Hey, we're going to give you subsidies. Whether you sell a bushel of corn or not, you're still going to get paid. We'll even pay you not to grow crops. But who really pays? The government has to take from you and me to give to that farmer.

Recently, a news report said that the farm subsidy program could safely be cut by $20 billion, but that neither political party was brave enough to tackle it. Slick Willie, knowing full well there is no need for a farm subsidy program, nevertheless goes to Iowa, panders to the farmers, and says that as long as he's president, the farm subsidy program will not be cut.

The farmers aren't ashamed. The giant corporations getting tax abatements so they can evade paying their fair share aren't ashamed either. They're in Washington fighting tooth and nail to get as many handouts as they can. When Lee Iacocca won the bailout for Chrysler, was he bashful about it? Hell, no—that gigantic act of welfare made him a star.

When I began railing against welfare, fraud was the hot issue. Back then, you couldn't pick up the paper without reading about some welfare queen who had managed to acquire real estate and a Cadillac while on the dole. If you pointed it out, you were called a racist. But the truth is that whites make up most of the welfare rolls. If cutting welfare will hurt anybody, whites will suffer most. Many years ago, a U.S. senator told me, "The loss to fraud in welfare is incalculable. Maybe it's better we don't know how much it costs us—we'd all have massive heart attacks if we did." That man was Barry Goldwater, of Arizona, among the most maligned public figures of his era. Naturally, he was right.

We don't read much about welfare fraud these days, which might lead you to assume that it's no longer a problem. Don't kid yourself. I just read that federal officials estimate food-stamp fraud alone costs the government $1 billion a year. Imagine that, just one little subcategory of welfare theft adds up to not one fortune but several.

The fraud goes on unabated because the bureaucracies that run our federal and state welfare programs are the most inept, disorganized, corrupt ones around. Why do you think that is? Because nobody truly believes welfare is a good thing. Nobody believes it will ever end poverty. In fact, it perpetuates it by allowing people to get by without ever making an effort in their own behalf. We don't want to think about that painful truth, and so the system festers in the dark, like a sore.

Now we're finally at the crossroads where welfare is concerned. The Republicans want to cut programs, so that we can cut the deficit, so that the American taxpayer won't have to pay quite as much in taxes as he does now. United States Representative John Kasich, of Ohio, is absolutely right. We either do something now or there will be catastrophe ahead. And that catastrophe is going to make the Depression of the 1930s look slight by comparison. If we do nothing, there won't be enough money to save all the people who will require saving.

But what, realistically, can we do? Callers expect that I'll be an absolutely heartless hard-liner where welfare is concerned, but I'm not. Anybody who needs a temporary hand should be helped. No doubt about it. And then there are those who simply will never be able to fend for themselves. We can't let people starve.

But I don't believe farmers need welfare. The farm subsidy program should be stopped this minute. The welfare payments that go to industry, by virtue of various tax breaks and tax abatements, should also end at once.

I believe that any able-bodied person without children should receive welfare only for a short, specific amount of time. They have to take responsibility for finding a job. They should be offered the chance to enter some kind of training program. If they flunk out, no more welfare. If they receive training, they *have* to find a job. Benefits to them should be cut off, after a period of time—sixty days, ninety days. Let's see how they react to the incentive.

Beyond that, though, I don't see a solution. Once a child is born, we can't let it starve or go without a home or medical care. A child with the misfortune of having been born to irresponsible moochers shouldn't be made to suffer any more than can be helped. If there were no generous welfare system, would that child even have been born? I doubt it. Which, in a way, makes us responsible for its existence. And so we pay and pay and pay. Every illegitimate, impoverished, state-dependent child in America today is the living legacy of the damned stupid and cruel vanity of LBJ and the rest of those who thought they could wipe out poverty forever.

# How We Pay for the Gun That's Pointed at Us

♦

THOUGH WE ALL MOAN ABOUT THE TAXES WE HAVE TO PAY, MOST people think of them the way they think of bad weather—nasty, but part of the natural order of things and beyond anybody's control. Everybody knows the famous line about nothing being as sure as death and taxes. Not so well known is the wisdom expressed by the great Supreme Court Chief Justice John Marshall, who said: "The power to tax involves the power to destroy."

We would all do well to remember that. Taxes aren't simply a nuisance or a minor burden to be silently borne, like a snowstorm. The power to tax is the mightiest force we allow our elected leaders to possess. It is meant to be applied wisely and in accordance with our wishes.

In the second half of this century, our leaders began to use taxes as a weapon to destroy us.

You give up your days and your energies to an employer or a customer, and in return they give you money—that's how the world works. So you should think of a dollar as what it truly is: a symbol of your time and labor. When you spend those dollars to provide the things you want and need, you're actually spending your own sweat, your own abilities, your own span on this planet.

And that's a sensible system, one we can all live with. But

then there are taxes. Having come together as a nation, we agree to surrender part of our livelihoods to pay for what we need done but cannot do on an individual basis. We need armed forces, for instance. We need highways. Harbors. Trash collection. Police and firemen. Schools. Food inspectors. The Secret Service. Of course, we need to fund the branches of federal government dictated by the Constitution, and the bureaucracy to carry out their tasks.

Nobody objects to that. Americans are willing to carry their share of a necessary burden, we've proven over and over again.

Except for a brief period during the Civil War, federal income taxes did not even exist until the passage of the Sixteenth Amendment, in 1913. Prior to that time, the government raised its operating funds with tariffs, excise taxes, sales taxes, import duties, and so on.

Even when the federal income tax started, most people didn't pay it, because only those earning $3,000 or so a year were taxed. Not many people cleared that hurdle back then. Prior to 1943, people were trusted to pay their taxes by March 15 of the following year. In other words, on March 15, 1926, you had to fork over what you owed on 1925's earnings.

That changed because of World War II's enormous demands on the federal budget. A Democrat (naturally) named Beardsley Ruml, who was chairman of the Federal Reserve Bank in New York, devised what became known as the Ruml Plan, which instituted the new concept of withholding taxes from payrolls.

That, in my opinion, was our downfall. Because if we still had to write a check to the IRS every year to pay our taxes, we'd have a much firmer idea of exactly how much we were paying. And we'd know enough to squawk when the bite got too big. I bet you can tell me exactly what you spend on car insurance or your mortgage. Can you say to the penny what you pay in taxes?

Once the money was taken from us before we ever saw it, and we started paying it in weekly or biweekly increments, we lost sight of what the income tax was really costing us. We began paying our taxes on the installment plan, which takes a big chunk of money and makes it seem like a little. It's a con game.

Of course, payroll deduction was necessary during wartime. But did they repeal it after the war was over? No—because once a politician gets his hands on your money, he'll never give it back. Is it any coincidence that once we paid off our wartime debt and got back on our feet, government began to grow huge? I don't think so. The stage was set by the early sixties; all that tax money was just lying around waiting to be spent.

Today, we find that our taxes are being squandered by a bureaucracy with no incentive to spend our money as prudently as we ourselves dole it out. So the bureaucracy grows huge: about one-fifth of the American workforce is now in the employ of some form of government—more than work in manufacturing. And government doesn't produce one damn thing, doesn't earn one damn dollar.

Why *should* the officeholders and bureaucrats value our money? They didn't have to earn it. And if they spend what we've given them and still need more, they don't have to make do, like the rest of us. They can just demand new or higher taxes. If your checking account is empty, can you go to your boss and order him to refill it? Can you demand that he borrow money to put in your pocket? I can't either, but the federal government does just that. The most disgusting part is that they claim to do this in *our* name!

Government waste and indifference to wage earners isn't the worst of it, however. The biggest sin, the absolute disgrace, was when our leaders decided that they'd do a little social engineering with our money. They decided on their own that some people had more money than they needed and others had not enough—and so they'd take from you and me and give it away. They call them "transfer payments" to disguise their true nature, and they now cost us $300 billion a year for poverty relief alone! Add to that programs like farm subsidies, corporate tax breaks, and good old-fashioned political pork—now you know what Marshall meant when he used the word "destroy."

The government can't give anybody money, because it has no money to give. Every dollar it gives away is a dollar it has taken. Even that's not quite true. Remember, our national debt is $4.7 trillion dollars. Do you know what a trillion *is?* A thousand billion. Our debt increases $38,158 every four seconds. So figure it out—how long does it take the federal government to go through the money you personally turn over?

The culprit in all this is easy to name. It was the tax-happy, spend-happy socialists of the Democratic party of the sixties and seventies. See a problem? Create an "entitlement" program, meaning one that requires not a single infusion of money but rather funding in perpetuity. Did LBJ ask you if you'd mind handing some of your money over to a new army of bureaucrats and the freeloaders they'd serve? He didn't ask me.

Who suffers most from current tax policies? The people who are breaking their backs to pay a mortgage and insurance and tuition, the people who work hard but then want to enjoy the fruits of their labor—without having government come along and mug them every time they manage to save a few bucks. In 1950, we paid an average of two percent of our income to the federal government. Today, every dollar you earn from January until sometime in May goes directly into running your government. You don't see a nickel of it.

I hate tax cheats, but I can't say I'm surprised that the current madness inspires otherwise law-abiding Americans to defraud the system. The so-called underground economy helps people to evade an estimated $150 billion in taxes they should be paying. The next time somebody brags to me about getting paid under the table, I think I'll punch him in the mouth. I don't know if it's because he's unpatriotic or I'm jealous. The very fact that people brag about having "a cash business" tells me that nobody believes the IRS or the government is playing fair.

We have no idea of how much money we pay in taxes. I read recently that there are as many as two hundred different taxes and levies wielded by federal, state, and local governments. The IRS rulebook alone runs to almost fifteen thousand pages. Taxes are sneaky and insidious. For instance, we think of the income tax as the main one, but how about the 7.5 percent you pay for Social Security? Your employer is required to match that payment, so it comes out to *15 percent* of your wages gone to Social Security.

The bottom line is this: Every year the federal government collects about $1.3 trillion in taxes. They use the word "collects" so it sounds as though they're owed that money, but they get it only because we've agreed to give it. It still isn't enough to cover what Uncle Sam spends in a year. We come up $200 billion short.

Just think of what $1.3 trillion could do if it were left in the hands of the people who earn it. Think of all the goods and services you'd purchase with the money now going to taxes. Think of all the certificates of deposit and mutual funds and shares of stock and business partnerships that would be bought if we kept the money we gave up to the government.

Letting our money do its work in the free market would be an efficient and fair way of redistributing wealth. The current coercive, wasteful method—allowing government to run the show—is a disaster. And so many of our problems— from the national debt to a weak dollar to intrusive, inept bureaucracy—would be solved by simply cutting off the government's allowance. By fixing the tax law.

The flat tax, in my opinion, is the only way to fix things. It would make the tax codes fair. It would allow us to disband the IRS, which is secretive, evil, and incompetent. It would instantly make government cheaper to run. It might put some accountants out of work, but they won't starve.

Our new tax system would be one-tiered—no two or three levels of percentage. We'd all pay a maximum of twenty percent of our income, end of story. If you earn a million this year, you pay $200,000, no loopholes or exemptions. If you earn $20,000, you hand over $4,000.

The odds against the flat tax are large, though. The Democrats don't want to give up their power to transform society as they see fit. And even though they lost control of the Congress, they have enough votes to block it. Slick Willie would veto it anyway. The only way we'll get a fair deal on our taxes is if this year the Republicans win even greater margins in both houses of the Congress *and* get one of their own in the White House. And even then, we might not get the type of flat tax that we really need. The propaganda that has been churned out by the Democrats is going to be hard to combat.

I recall that when I first began talking about the flat tax, people either didn't know what I was talking about or they thought I was a loony. Well, some of them still think I'm a loony, but now most people know what the flat tax means. Maybe there's hope yet.

# *Crime and Punishment (Ha Ha Ha)*

——— ◆ ———

OKAY—WHO AMONG US ARE WE GOING TO SACRIFICE TO THE beasts today?

Let's see. Mr. Jackson, we're going to allow you to be murdered this morning. It's going to happen when you open your grocery store. Sorry about that. Now . . . Miss Cohen, you're going to be raped in your own apartment. Beaten up a little, too. Can't be helped. Mr. Spinelli, you'll be robbed at gunpoint at your garage this afternoon, and Mr. Perez, Mrs. Heath, and Mr. and Mrs. Rosen—you'll all have your cars stolen tonight. The Cranes, the Webers, the Bergs, and the Truscotts, all your houses will be burglarized while you're at work. Mr. and Mrs. Moore, your ten-year-old is going to be kidnapped and sexually tortured. Our apologies. Hope she gets over it soon.

Sound sick?

Yes, it does, but day in and day out, that is essentially our society's position on crime.

Every time a career criminal commits a new outrage, he is trying to tell us something important about himself. He's declaring it loud and clear. He's saying this: "I kill. I rob. I rape. I molest children. I sell dope. I am putting you good people on notice—this is what I do. This is who I *am*. Look at me! I'm not going to live by your rules. With me on the

loose, your wife, your children, your property, your life—
none of them are safe. You can lock me away for a little
while, but the instant you set me free, I'll strike again."

They're yelling this into our faces!

And how do we respond? We play deaf. We pretend we
didn't hear a thing. We act as if they didn't really mean it.
They *couldn't* really mean it, could they? Nice people don't
act like that.

What a bunch of patsies we are!

I've talked to lots of police officers and others in the criminal justice system, both in New York and Los Angeles. They
all tell me the same thing, that a small percentage of the
population keeps committing the same crimes over and over.
The streets aren't swarming with criminals. But there are
enough of them on the loose to create absolute mayhem and
anarchy among the good people. I just read (thanks to a
newspaper column written by my hero, Thomas Sowell) that
a study of more than one hundred thousand former prisoners
showed that sixty-three percent of them were rearrested for
serious crimes, including two thousand murders. If we would
put these monsters away, and put them away permanently,
the crime rate in this country would plunge. The ideal solution, of course, would be simply to execute these savages.
But, no—only the Ayatollah Cockamamie does that. Only
wackos do that.

Wrong—wackos go on allowing the decimation of the de-
fenseless, law-abiding population. That's what wackos do.

I remember taking my children to a zoo when they were
young. First we visited the petting zoo, and there were little
lambs and goats and bunny rabbits, docile, peaceful creatures. The children loved being able to touch the animals
and get down on the ground with them. Then we went over
to the big-cat house, where they kept the lions, tigers, panthers, leopards, and cheetahs. And my younger son asked
me, "Hey, Dad, why can't we pet *these* animals?" I said,
"Because they're dangerous." He then asked, "Why are they
dangerous?" I replied, "Because nature has made them that
way. They will bite you, they will chew you up, and then
they will eat you. They can't help it. That's just how they
were made." And it took him a while to understand that

there are some animals you can pet and play with, and some you must fear and avoid. That some will lick your hand, and others will bite it off. But eventually, the lesson sunk in.

Now, if a six-year-old can comprehend that, why can't a society of enlightened, educated, intelligent adults?

On my Saturday network show recently, I talked about the case of a fifty-one-year-old fiend in Toms River, New Jersey, who had been arrested for—and indeed, pleaded guilty to— having attempted to sodomize an eleven-year-old boy. This individual had previously sodomized and murdered an eight-year-old boy in 1977. For that he served a grand total of eight years in prison, one for each year of the tiny, trusting life he had desecrated and snuffed out.

And what sentence did this vermin get for his latest evil act?

Three years.

What sense does that make? Is there some magic that a jail cell performs? You take a mutant, a monster—and that's what this skunk is, a monster—you put him in a jail, and somehow he comes out a law-abiding citizen? Did the air in prison heal him? The food? The fine company?

I want to know why there's no death penalty for devils like him. Barring that, I want to know why, once a person has served notice on society, we won't take measures to make sure he can't get his vicious paws on any more innocent lives.

I remember the case of a worm out in Los Angeles who had murdered his seven-year-old stepson—a brutal, brutal murder—and it turned out that he had killed like this before. I had many friends in the Los Angeles County Sheriff's Department, and I asked one, "Why in heaven's name was this guy let out?" He said, "Because we have a criminal code. And you look at the criminal code and it says: For this crime a person gets this sentence. Mitigating circumstances will reduce the sentence." I said, "What are mitigating circumstances?" He said, "Whatever sob story his attorney can sell to a jury or to a judge." Did you know that three out of four convicted criminals don't serve any time at all? Or that nationwide, criminals serve less than thirty-seven percent of their sentences? All true.

## Whose Government Is This, Anyway?

When I came to New York, there was the case of a young woman who had been brutally murdered—her body left on the roof of a building—by a person who was allegedly a piano tuner. I was outraged over the case. It turned out that five years prior to my arrival in New York, the same demon had committed virtually the same crime. This deviant's name was Charlie, and back then Charlie had convinced the head-shrinkers and social workers in the New York state prison system that he was suddenly an okay guy. They said: "Charlie's come a long way. We like Charlie." Like Charlie? He left a twenty-one-year-old girl dead on a roof—strangled her to death—and you want to let him out again? "No," they insisted, "Charlie's all right." But Charlie was *not* all right! Charlie was programmed to kill. Charlie all but told us, "I am not meant to live among women." But we wouldn't listen. And so we gave Charlie the chance to kill again. He was glad to take it.

I talked about this on the air, and this girl's mother called me and wrote to me. She said, "Mr. Grant—you're the only one who understands. You're the only one who cares. People shrug their shoulders and say my daughter's just another victim."

I'm going to tell you something not many people realize. There is one reason and one reason only that our government—*any* humane government—exists. Mankind created government in order to protect the lives and property of ordinary people, so that we can live our days as we choose with our physical beings and hard-earned possessions intact. Read the Preamble to our own Constitution. It says that document was adopted in order to "establish justice, insure domestic tranquility, provide for the common defence, promote the general welfare . . ."

The great philosophers of the Enlightenment knew that a free society could not survive unless its members could be kept safe from predators. Back then, remember, there was no criminal justice system with the sophistication and reach of what we have today. Providing protection and security for the people was the core responsibility and sole justification of our nation, then and now.

And so I say that our leaders have absolutely no right to

spend even one nickel on frivolities—supporting avant-garde playwrights, studying the mating habits of the snail darter, providing free postage to congressmen—until they have made us safe in our homes and streets.

How can that great goal be accomplished? Now, of course, I believe in the death penalty, and it seems to be the only rational answer to certain types of crime. But if the bleeding hearts continue to have their way, the death penalty will be very difficult to use in most states. And even when it is used, in places like Texas and Alabama, the average time between the crime and the execution is twelve to fourteen years.

If we lived in a sane world, here's who would get the death penalty:

All murderers. No exceptions.

All those convicted of attempted murder. You know, I have to laugh. Let's say somebody shoots you. He shoots you *six times*. Miraculously, you survive. Maybe you have a strong constitution. Maybe the bullets missed your vitals. Maybe the shooter just had lousy aim or he was so high on drugs and drink that he couldn't fire straight. He'll get an easy sentence! Despite the fact that he tried to kill you! For some reason, we reward criminals with lousy aim. It's idiotic. His intention was the same as the murderer's. And so he, too, deserves death as his punishment.

Pedophiles should be executed, for two reasons. One, they're extremely dangerous, and many times they'll kill their little victims. Psychiatrists argue over why they do that—maybe it's because they blame the victim for enticing them. Who the hell cares about their excuse? They did it, so they should die. The second reason they should get death is simply because they can't be deterred from striking over and over again. I learned something when I visited Vacaville, in California, which is the site of the sex criminal prison. I was told that there's no cure for this evil perversion.

Arsonists should also get the death penalty. If no one dies in the arson, it's a miracle, and no credit to the torch. They endanger innocent lives by their crime, so they, like killers with bad aim, should die.

Rapists, too, should be executed. Like child molesters, there's no reforming them. They have this obsessive-compulsive behavior, and obsessive-compulsive behavior can only be ended by death. If keeping them in jail served any purpose, I'd say okay, keep them in jail. But it does not serve any purpose.

Spies and traitors should get the death penalty. The Walkers. Mr. Ames. They stole secrets and sold them to the enemy. They endangered the very nation we love. So they should fry.

I wouldn't give death to drunk drivers, though I'm amazed that they get off so lightly. There, again you have compulsive behavior. I don't think a person says, "I'm going to get blind drunk, and I'm going to get behind the wheel of a car, and I'm going to wreck the car and kill people." But their compulsion to get drunk overcomes them.

I don't want the death penalty for burglars, muggers, embezzlers, and others who commit crimes against property. I'll even spare the lives of those bastards who assault, rob people at gunpoint, and sell drugs. But they should be punished severely. They should be but away for a long, long time. And there should be truth in sentencing. If the sentence is five to ten years, then that person should serve a minimum of five years. That's what five to ten *means*. None of this time off for criminals who behave well. They didn't behave when it counted—that's why they're in jail!

# My War on Drugs
# (A Modest Proposal)

———— ◆ ————

BACK IN THE SEVENTIES, I WAS AT A PARTY ALONG WITH SOME POLI
ticians, dignitaries, and a member of the New York City
Council. He was accompanied by his girlfriend (he left his
wife home that night). At one point in the evening, he tapped
me on the shoulder and asked me to pass a lit joint to his
mistress.

Now, I've never used marijuana or any other recreational
drug. I've never smoked cigarettes. A drink or two once in a
great while is about it for me. But I'm a polite guy, and he
asked nicely, so I took the joint, holding it as far from my
face as possible, and handed it to her. I didn't want that
smoke anywhere near me. It stunk.

Later, that moment haunted me. Here was an elected official of the largest city in America who felt completely at ease
engaging in an illegal act in front of other people who held
government positions. He was operating with the certainty
that no one in the room would make a fuss over what he
was doing. He would not have felt as comfortable stealing
someone's wallet, say, or scrawling graffiti on the wall. But
he broke the drug law without a worry. And this was long
before Slick Willie was caught with a reefer in his big mouth.

That's when the futility of our effort to wipe out drugs
really sunk in for me. Everyone can see the absolute devasta-

tion drug use has caused in America—death, disease, most of our street crimes, an unbelievable burden on police, broken individuals and families, sky-high medical costs, prison over-crowding. We all know how it drains tax money from the federal, state, and city budgets. No one knows this better than a member of the City Council. And yet this joker was puffing away, high as a kite, and nobody in the room blinked. Even *I* had a hand in it.

Some public figures say that if only we improved conditions in the inner cities and provided rehabilitation for addicts, the problem would disappear. Nonsense. America has always had poor people and ghettos. But most people living in poverty do *not* become drug addicts. To suggest that poverty is responsible for addiction is an insult to all those poor people of the past and present who never turned to an easy escape from the hard work of improving their lives. And we've all heard of the nice middle-class suburban types who fall in love with drugs.

As for rehab, well, we've seen it work once in a while. But only for those individuals who really and truly want to get off drugs. Tomorrow, we could send every drug addict in America to the Betty Ford Clinic in a limousine, and the majority of them would *still* go right back on crack or heroin or whatever. You don't "cure" junkies the way you do people with cancer. One hundred percent of the people with cancer *want* to be cured. Most drug users want one thing only—more drugs.

Then there are those who say that stronger attempts to stop the supply of drugs from crossing our borders will do the trick. That and stiffer sentences for pushers and users. More nonsense. Every week we hear about the tons of cocaine and heroin and marijuana that have been intercepted. But then we're told that's just a small fraction of what comes into this country. If tons and tons of dope are coming into the United States, it's only because they are being consumed. You can't name me one instance where an illegal craving hasn't succeeded in getting satisfaction, regardless of the laws. Prohibition. Laws against pornography. Prostitution. The outcome is always the same—people who want it will get it. They don't care about prison, either. If you made burglary a capital offense tomorrow, all our burglars would turn to other ways of making a living. Even the death penalty wouldn't scare a junkie off drugs.

Some of my good conservative friends say we ought to become even more aggressive against the foreign suppliers of drugs—bomb the Colombian cocaine fields, poison the poppy and marijuana fields, withhold foreign aid from supplier countries until they clean up their act. Forget it. None of that will make a dent. These countries can barely wipe their noses without help, and they're going to solve *our* problems?

Fact is, even *I* don't have a good solution to the drug mess. I do have a solution, though, but it doesn't sound pretty, even to me.

First thing we do is offer help to any drug user who says he wants to kick. We give them one chance, and if they don't take it, well, it's their choice. We don't owe addicts endless indulgence. We aren't obligated to let them rob us, kill us, take up our hospital beds and jail cells and public housing forever and ever.

Then, we start making all illegal drugs available to whoever wants them. Not only available, but absolutely free of charge.

There's just one catch. Most of the dope we dispense will be perfectly fine and normal, just what the junkie ordered. But *some* of it will contain a chemical that will instantly kill the user. It's the Russian roulette program: Maybe you'll get nine perfectly blissful fixes, but the tenth one will put you out of your misery for good. You'll get a high that lasts for eternity.

Now, like a lot of my proposals, that sounds shocking. But all the pleasant, humane, nice-guy solutions to drug addiction have failed miserably, and we have to admit that sooner or later. Under my proposal, those who genuinely want to get off drugs will have a good chance of doing so. If we make them face this choice—kick drugs or die—it just might work. Those who would risk certain death just to get high will never be cured. After a while, they won't be around to burglarize, to kill, to maim, to drive their cars into our cars. In short, we will be rid of people who obviously don't want to live anyway.

Even if you despise my modest proposal, there's one thing
you must grant—it shows a little imagination. That's more
than I can say for anything that has come from the psychologists and social workers who have been trying for the past
thirty years to solve the drug problem.

For me, it all comes down to one question: Why is it that
the nonjunkies among us—the people who are productive
and healthy and law-abiding, the Americans who take responsibility for their own welfare and then pay taxes to ensure the welfare of others—why is it that *we* have to suffer
because somebody else is weak? Why is there no end to what
we're required to do to help people who won't help themselves? You wouldn't conduct your own life that way. If
someone took endless advantage of your generosity, at some
point you'd say "Enough!" and stop being so wonderful. So
why can't we, as a society, see the wisdom of making the
same kind of stand?

# *The Worst Job in America Today*

——— ◆ ———

IF YOU HIRED A PLUMBER, YOU'D LET HIM DO HIS JOB IN PEACE, without telling him when to use his wrenches and how. If you hired a stockbroker, you'd allow him to make your trades without watching him every second, waiting for him to screw up. When you go to a restaurant, you don't stand in the kitchen ordering the chef around and telling him how to cook your veal chop.

And when your plumber or your broker or a restaurant chef or anybody else you hire does a good job, you're appreciative. You're grateful and you show it.

So what's the deal with police officers?

They're certainly more important than any plumber, broker, or chef. They enforce the Constitution by protecting your right to live and pursue happiness without interference. They do more to uphold the Constitution than all the Supreme Court justices, judges, attorney generals, legislators, and lawyers who have ever lived—and they do it for less money, twenty-four hours a day, seven days a week. They *risk* more, too. They put their own lives in jeopardy to keep ours safe.

And yet they are under siege by the American public. Their enemies libel, persecute, and hound them. Even worse, normal citizens are aloof, disdainful, mistrustful. They betray cops by their indifference, by their unwillingness to support them vocally.

This, to me, is where our society's suicidal tendencies come through loudest. For we are a nation of laws. How we treat law officers is a reflection of how we feel about our country. Too many Americans have lost faith and confidence in our system, and their ambivalence shows in their attitude about cops. If you don't believe in America, then you don't believe in its laws. And you take it out on the men and women in blue.

To be a cop today is really asking for trouble. We put them in uniform, give them a badge and a gun, and make them swear to uphold the laws that protect society. We throw them out there among the most vile, animalistic criminals the human race has ever spawned. Then we tie their hands behind their backs and second-guess every move they make. If there's a dispute between the police and a lawbreaker, we hem and haw over whose side to take. Every miscreant is permitted human failings, but we insist that cops be perfect. If there's a benefit of the doubt to be given, we automatically give it to whoever opposes the police.

And still they soldier on. It's a miracle that anybody becomes a police officer today. Would *you* do a job that's dangerous, difficult, *and* absolutely thankless? One in which you were practically guaranteed disrespect, no matter how well you did it?

Of course, we all know about police officers who abuse their power. Or those who are simply unfit psychologically for the demands of the work. You can say the same of the medical profession or newspaper reporters or lawyers or others in positions of public trust. But we don't automatically mistrust *all* doctors, and so on, as a result. Bad cops are a very small minority. We use police corruption or brutality as an excuse to malign and mistreat all cops, even the best ones.

I have come to know a great many police officers. I know one named Gary Spath, who until recently protected the people of Teaneck, New Jersey. He did more than that, too; he also volunteered his time to work with poor kids from that town. One night he got a call that some teenagers were fighting, and one, the caller said, had a gun. Spath found the guy

and ordered him to stop. Instead, this sixteen-year-old *man*—
and I call him that because he was mature enough to already
have a criminal record—took off. Spath chased him into the
night, caught up, and ordered him to freeze. Instead, the miscreant reached into his coat pocket. Spath fired one shot,
which missed, and the suspect ran again. Spath caught him
a second time and again, ordered him to freeze. Again, the
guy reached into his pocket. Spath's second shot did not
miss. The suspect died. When police searched him, they
found a starter pistol that had been converted to fire real .22-
caliber bullets.

Now, what would cause somebody to run after a police
officer ordered him to stop? Obviously, only someone with
a reason to flee would do so. But people today no longer
recognize the authority of a police officer. By current thinking, a cop has no more right than you or I to tell anybody to
stop and answer questions or, if necessary, to be frisked.
These germs refuse to acknowledge that the law allows police
any powers beyond what the average citizen possesses. If
this kind of thinking spreads, our laws themselves will be
endangered.

So did the people of Teaneck support Spath in this effort to
keep them safe? Some of them did, but not all—the shooting
sparked a full-scale riot. That's not all. Gary Spath was arrested and charged with reckless manslaughter. He was
demonized by the people of Teaneck who would take the
side of lawlessness against that of the law. After a long and
arduous trial, Spath was acquitted. But he was so devastated
by the experience that he left the force. Who will suffer? Not
Spath—his ordeal is behind him now. The rest of the
Teaneck force will never get over the feeling that the people
they protect don't value their lives. In the end, the law-
abiding people of Teaneck will suffer most.

I speak out in behalf of cops on my show all the time.
Once I supported officers at a particular precinct here in New
York City, and they came by and thanked me effusively. At
the time I thought, what's so unusual about a guy on the
radio supporting the police? But they told me, "Bob, you just
listen, or read the papers. You just look around at your breth-
ren in the media and tell us how many of you guys really

support policemen." It still happens—a cop will come up to me and say, "Bob, I've been on the job for eighteen years. Please don't stop talking about us. We need you." I'm not exaggerating one bit. It breaks my heart to hear these big, tough guys, who risk everything to serve us, sounding so discouraged.

It's fashionable today among pseudointellectuals to be anticop. They think that it raises their stature to scorn those who devote their lives to upholding the law. But the law is all that keeps those phony weasels alive and free to speak their minds.

The second that cops stop doing their jobs, this country will begin to die.

# The Lowest Class

———— ◆ ————

I AM A MAN WITH NO ILLUSIONS, AT LEAST WHERE POLITICIANS ARE concerned. You people, the general public, are still very naive about the politician class. You don't understand that, with rare exception, politicians are thinking about one thing only: how they stand in the polls. Former Democratic party chief Larry O'Brien, in his advice to politicians way back in 1960, said it best: "The first duty of a politician is to get elected. The second duty of a politician is to get reelected. The third duty is to get reelected again."

I don't think that because New Jersey Governor Christine Whitman returned to my program after the *New York* magazine controversy, she's a wonderful person. There are very few politicians who are wonderful people. By virtue of what they do, they *can't* be wonderful people. They are cynical. They are not to be trusted. Very rarely does their word mean anything—and that goes for members of both parties.

So how does a sensible person decide which candidate to back, which party to join? Here's how *I* do it. The basic political philosophy of one party is far closer to mine than the other, and that's why I'm a Republican—not because I think Republicans are such great guys and Democrats are such louses. When you come down to it, just about every person who runs for office is a louse; you just vote for the louse who expresses a political philosophy closer to your way of thinking. And the Republicans tax less and are less interested in interfering in my life, and that's why I'm a Republican. Again, I stress—not because they're peachy-keen and the Democrats are lousy. (Of course, Democrats *are* lousy, but that goes without saying.)

Despite all that's happened, I will continue to endorse candidates—I think it's important that I do that—but I will never again get so involved in somebody's campaign that they can hurt me. Once was enough. I was involved in the George Pataki campaign, and in spite of what I've just said, I still would like to think that George Pataki wouldn't betray me or sell me out. But I'm not rock-solid certain he wouldn't—he's a politician. So I have to keep reminding myself: A politician is thinking only about getting reelected. And if you're excess baggage, they will jettison you before you can say, "Let's be heard."

There are some who will cut you loose immediately. They do it just because that's the way they are. Spineless and opportunistic, like viruses. There are others, like Ronald Reagan, who would fold only because the Jim Bakers of the world convince them to fold. We don't have Henry Clays around anymore, leaders who say, "I would rather be right than be President." We don't have people who say, "Well, listen—I'm not gonna turn my back on Bob Grant."

In fact, politicians today are worse than ever before.

In the old days, a real pol—an alderman, a councilman—would say to everybody he met, "Hey, Chippo! What are the people saying?" And somebody would reply, "Well, you know, they don't like what you said about so-and-so."

"Oh, yeah? Gee, what'd they say?"

"Well . . ." And then maybe the pol might change his view, or he might go out and confront the people who disagree with him and convince them that he's right. That's leadership. Now politicians have perpetual polling. Once a campaign gets underway, they're having hour-by-hour public-opinion surveys. "And does this play well?" the pol now asks his pollster. "Ooh," the pollster will say, "they didn't like that." "Well, let's change that." It's minute-by-minute market testing, constant waffling to appease the voters.

Now, you ask—what's wrong with that? Shouldn't the pols listen to the people?

Well, the people may not be right. They can't be right all the time, especially when "the people" believe contradictory things. If a politician says, I believe in the flat tax, and he gets polls saying some people don't like the flat tax, he has a choice: he can either drop the flat tax, or he can stick to his guns and try to convince the public that he's right—if he really believes that he's right. There are two ways to go: One way reveals you're just a politician trying to get elected; the other way is for the statesmanlike individual who believes that he has a duty to lead the people in the right direction. That's what they're supposed to do. That's what presidents are supposed to do. And yet it doesn't work out.

So here's my advice when it comes to politicians. Don't get carried away by their personalities or by what you perceive as their characters. Rather, study what they say they intend to do if they're elected. If you call a plumber and when he arrives you don't like the way he dresses or the way he talks, do you send him away? If he's a good plumber, and he's going to do the job better than another guy who may dress better and talk nicer, whom do you pick? If you're smart, you pick the good plumber. You should forget about the pol's smile, forget about the charisma, forget about the image. Study what they stand for. It's what they stand for politically that counts. That is the *only* thing that counts.

Don't ask a politician to promise you that he's a good guy and you will never be deceived.

Of course, we *have* had politicians who were statesmen, dependable leaders instead of poll watchers. Dwight Eisenhower, who had some definite ideas about where to take the country, didn't care about his image. In fact, he pretended he was a little on the addled side—a muddling-type guy, to look at him. His syntax was terrible. But he had a program and he carried it out. He believed that we needed a national highway system and that the money from the gasoline tax should be dedicated to that. A lot of politicians said, "Well, *this* would be more popular, or *that* would be more popular, with the voters." But he said, "No, this is what we need." And now people look back and say, "Hey, thank God Dwight

Eisenhower did that." He's a good example of what I mean by leadership. He didn't argue with a lot of people. You know, Ike even played the part of the fool sometimes. But his policies prevailed. He may not have been the charismatic, handsome John Kennedy, but I think the legacy he left will prove to be more enduring than Kennedy's. Kennedy's legacy is not of substance but of emotion, and over the long haul, that's not what really counts.

Another great statesman of our time is the man who was once my all-time hero, Barry Goldwater. In the middle of a heated campaign, he had the courage to vote against the 1964 Civil Rights Act, because he believed that at least two of its seven provisions were unconstitutional and unfair. Naturally, he was slammed and called every slanderous name in the book, but now, looking back, some people say that Barry Goldwater had a point.

Goldwater also talked about Vietnam in no uncertain terms. He said, Look, if we're going to be there, we should beat the hell out of those guys. If we're not willing to do that, let's bring the troops home. Meanwhile, Lyndon Johnson kept saying, "Ah seek no wider war. We're not gonna get involved. I'm not gonna send American boys to die in Asia." As a result, the people gave Johnson a huge landslide victory. Goldwater carried only five states, and the Republicans went down to defeat with him. Goldwater's name became an epithet. And, yet, here was a man of great courage, a man who did not sacrifice his principles to win an election. And he lost to a fraud.

Goldwater was a decent man, too. I interviewed him on several occasions. He never put on airs. He wasn't pompous or full of himself, as some politicians are.

The third true leader we've known in recent history is Ronald Reagan. He had an agenda, he had a program, and people knew where he stood. Ronald Reagan said the Soviet Union was the Evil Empire, and everybody said, "Oh, how wrong. What a terrible, unsophisticated thing to say." Now we're looking back—I just saw a PBS documentary that says, yes, it *was* an evil empire.

I first met Ronald Reagan in late 1965. I had a show at the time on KABC in Los Angeles, and our producer, Gary

Miller, got a call from Bill Roberts of Spencer Roberts, the PR firm. He said, "Hey, Gary—how'd you like to have Bob Grant interview Ronald Reagan?" And Gary said, "Well, I don't know—I'll have to talk to Bob. You know that Bob doesn't really *do* show-business stuff." And Roberts said, "Hey, wait a minute, I don't want him to interview Ronald Reagan as an *actor*. He's a politician now—he's going to run for governor."

"Oh, *is* he?" Gary said. "Well, I'll talk to Bob."

Now, I was familiar with the political speech Ronald Reagan gave in 1964. It was so well-known that insiders simply called it "The Speech." I also knew that he had switched from being a liberal Democrat to a conservative Republican. But back then, when his guys said, "He's running for governor," everybody laughed.

Anyway, we scheduled Ronald Reagan. My show was on at night in those days, and he showed up wearing riding boots, riding pants, turtleneck sweater, and sports jacket. He looked like a movie star. He was fifty-five then and handsome, with blue eyes that danced. Here are the three things I remember most about our first encounter:

Number one, meeting him just made you feel good. I mean, no wonder he won so many elections, because he just seemed to light up a room.

Number two, I recall the undisguised cynicism of the people at KABC. They thought he was a joke. The program director, a couple of the engineers, even my own producer, said, "Yeah, yeah, he's running for governor—sure."

And the third thing I remember was how absolutely clumsy he was once we went on the air.

Now, you know the format of my show—I take phone calls. Well, I introduced Ronald Reagan, asked him a few questions, and then we went to the telephone lines. And I guess he had never had to do that kind of thinking on his feet before, because no sooner did he begin to speak than he was stumbling and fumbling all over the place. And I was covering for him—I was completing his answers, stepping in to make sense of what he was trying to say. You know, it's all ad-lib. People are throwing stuff at him: "What would you do about the University of California?" "What would you do with Mario Savio (who was carrying on then with the so-called Free Speech Movement)?"

"Well," he said, "well, I don't think that these people should be carrying on like that."

The caller fired back, "Don't you believe in freedom of speech?!"

And Reagan said, "Well, now, I, I, I—you know . . ."

So I stepped in and said, "Look, of course he believes in freedom of speech. But after all, we have to have some semblance of order and an atmosphere for learning up there, and right now there's only anarchy." I'm giving all these great answers to cover for him! Because I didn't want him to look bad.

Finally a woman caller came on the air and said, "Hey, you know what's wrong? You two guys oughta switch places! Mr. Reagan, you oughta be the host of the show, and Mr. Grant, *you* oughta run for governor!"

And I looked at Ronald Reagan's expression—I mean, he was just so hurt and dismayed. So, trying to smooth things over, I jumped back in and said, "Well, ma'am, I'm certainly not qualified to run for governor."

To which she replied, "Well, *he* sure ain't!"

After two hours of that, the show ended, and he said, "You know, Mr. Grant"—he still called me Mr. Grant—"I will never forget how kind you were. I don't know how to thank you."

I said, "I'll tell you how you can thank me. When you win the primary, you can kick off your campaign against Pat Brown on my show." And he turned to his publicist and said, "Bill, we'll do that." And Bill smiled, as if to say, "Yeah, in a pig's ass we will."

Now, I was still being kind to Ronald Reagan when I said that he'd win the primary. Like *The Los Angeles Times* and *The San Francisco Chronicle* and nearly everybody else, I thought that George Christopher, the mayor of San Francisco, would win the election. I *wanted* Christopher to win the primary, for only one reason: I felt he had the best chance to beat Pat Brown. I know you readers might be disappointed in me, because you might think that sounds awfully expedient, coming from a man of great conviction. But I also feel that there's a pragmatic streak in me—you might call it something else—that says we've got to back the candidate who has the best chance of winning.

However, I'm proud to tell you that when the primary came along, I voted for Ronald Reagan. Even though there were six other candidates in the field and the L.A. *Times* picked him to come in sixth. Lo and behold, the next day, when the results came in, Ronald Reagan won easily. And, yes, he did keep his promise to return to my show.

Throughout his career in public office, Reagan, like Ike, remained a very self-effacing man. No airs at all. If anything, he may have been too humble. I recall in 1976, when he was challenging Gerry Ford for the presidential nomination, Reagan's people scheduled him for an interview with me at Republican County Leader George Clark's office in Brooklyn. I had my tape recorded, and I asked him all the questions I wanted to ask. Finally, because I knew he had an important meeting to go to, I brought the interview to an end. And he stood there—waiting for me to excuse him. That had never happened to me before, nor has it happened since. At some point in an interview, your typical politician always glances at his watch and says, "Listen, I'm sorry—I gotta go." Sometimes they just turn and walk off. Reagan stood there, waiting for me to tell him I had all I needed and it was all right to leave. I never forgot that. George Clark noticed it, too. George said, "What a guy. I saw him standing there, waiting for you to tell him it was over."

My last encounter with Ronald Reagan came in 1988, when I celebrated my fortieth anniversary in radio. As a surprise, my producers scheduled various well-known people to call in and congratulate me. Suddenly, a recorded message came on the air—and it was the president of the United States saying, "I salute you, Bob Grant, for your dedication, *blah blah blah.*"

I think Ronald Reagan was an unusual leader and politician because he was such a very decent fellow. Maybe that's why Nancy became so tough, because she felt that she had to make up for the fact that Ronnie was such a good soul. She herself said that she had to be the way she was because Ronnie is such a softie, and people take advantage of him.

She's a great, loyal wife. I mean, she has her ways—look at what she did to Ollie North. There was no need for her to go into Virginia and tell people that Ollie North was a liar. And I believe that's why he didn't beat Chuck Robb. But she said in effect, "Hey, look—he didn't do right by my husband, and so I'll get him." Like most people, she wants to retaliate; she can be vindictive. But Ronald Reagan doesn't have a vindictive bone in his body. No malice at all.

It's amazing that he was able to withstand what we charitably call the political process of running for the highest office in the land. He succeeded for two reasons. First, America was ready for his political philosophy. And second, the guy makes a great speech. Nobody makes a greater speech. He may not be good at questions and answers, although he comes up with his quips. But when he speaks, people sense his decency.

The people liked Ronald Reagan—not in spite of his self-effacing nature but because of it. Having been alone with him, having seen him before he was elected to his first office, I feel that I know his essence. He's a good, simple man. And I say he is "simple" not in a pejorative sense, but in the way that the good people of this world usually are simple. Not simple-minded.

He won because he could go into New Hampshire, a small state where TV coverage is not really all that important—a state where whistle-stops, bus stops, luncheonettes, street corners *are* important—and light up the state. He radiated a sense of well-being that made you feel good. What everybody remembers is the time when, at a rally, some heckler was trying to usurp the mike and Reagan got a little exasperated and said, "Look—I *paid* for this microphone." And people liked that. They like it when a good, decent guy speaks up and strikes back.

Now, that was the real Ronald Reagan. But I also have a story about the fake Ronald Reagan.

Joan Quigley was a nationally famous astrologer even before she became known as Nancy Reagan's personal star-watcher. And Joan wrote a book, went on a book tour, and was guest on my show. A very lovely lady. After we talked awhile, we went to the telephones and took calls from listeners, who would tell us their birthdays so Joan could tell them about themselves.

Now, the stars may tell Joan everything, but they didn't tell her that somebody in my control room had cooked up a little trick. We had Jay Diamond, who does impersonations, call doing Ronald Reagan's voice. So this caller said he was born on February 6, 1911. And she broke into a huge grin and said, "Oh, Mr. President, I *knew* it was you the minute you started talking. And, of course, Bob, you know he's an Aquarian, and that's why he went into government service. Aquarians like to serve . . ." And she went on and on. And after a minute I felt embarrassed, because we had no idea she'd fall for the gag so completely. I had a choice: I could either tell her that she had been tricked by an impersonator, and end up embarrassing her, or I could just let her go on believing that Reagan took the time to call my show to talk to her. And by this point she had been going on and on, "Oh, Mr. President, how nice of you to call. I can't tell you how much it means to me . . ."

So I did the honorable thing: I never said a word.

After the broadcast ended, she's picking up her hat and coat, and she turns to me and says, "What a wonderful interviewer you are. And wasn't it nice of the President to call? I'll never forget that." And I say, "Uh, well, uh, yes—uh, it was very nice." And it was.

# Perot and Con

——— ◆ ———

IF YOU STILL REQUIRE EVIDENCE OF HOW STUPID, GULLIBLE, AND sheeplike the American people can be, you need look no further than the little dictator with the big ears—H. Ross Perot.

I am dumbstruck when I realize that he'll be a factor in the presidential election this year, either through his own candidacy (God forbid) or that of some Perotite third-party hopeful.

He is a liar. He is a coward. He is a tyrant. He is a paranoid. He has delusions of grandeur. He proved all that and more last time around. But still, there are Americans who are looking to him for a signal or a sign of what they should do this year. It's depressing. He's a fake, phony fraud if ever there was one, and yet he is a possible factor in the race to choose a leader of the free world.

In 1992, despite the fact that he was on the verge of an electoral miracle (in some polls, remember, he was in second place), he suddenly dropped out of the campaign. People were mystified. Common sense would tell you that the guy had a screw loose. Then he rejoined the race, explaining that he had previously pulled out because if he hadn't, the Republicans were going to ruin his daughter's wedding. Preposterous! Oh, a few Democrats seemed to take his excuse seriously, but only because they knew a Perot candidacy would hurt Bush and help Clinton.

And *still* there were idiots out there who voted for Perot. There's nothing dumber than casting your vote for a third-party "protest" candidate. It's saying, "My opinion is insignificant, I know, and so I'll waste my only chance to actually determine the future course of events." It's saying, "I'd rather have one hundred percent of nothing than thirty or forty or fifty percent of something."

Ross Perot is an arrogant individual, who, I suppose, has every right to be—with a couple of billion dollars, why not? He doesn't have to curry favor with anybody, unless he wants to get elected. And why would he want to get elected? Because no matter how much money a person has, they still seek more power. That's why people who have hundreds of millions of dollars still strive to make more. Money and power are addictive.

Now, you can get just so much power out of your money. You can push around the people in your employ or your bankers or your greedy grandchildren, but that's about it. After that, you need the forces of government at your beck and call. Perot liked the power he had over the media, stimulating curiosity like few public figures in recent memory. And yet, what in heaven's name did he have to offer except a few clichés? I think that when it became obvious to him that maybe he really *could* be elected, he lost his courage. He turned tail because he knew if he were elected, then he'd have to put up.

He was like the great and powerful Wizard of Oz! You get behind the curtain and you see that he's nothing but a little old man frantically pulling levers. Did he offer even one practicable solution to any of our problems? Not that I remember.

I loathe the idea of a Perotite candidate in part because it can only hurt the Republicans. They're certainly not going to damage Slick Willie and the hard-core, left-wing, politically correct scumbags following him.

But the main reason I despair over the cult of Perot is because it reminds me of how brainless Americans are when it comes to politics. We are cursed with citizens who go through life looking for a messiah, a savior. I don't know what it is they're looking to be saved *from*. I think the Republicans have been doing what was thought undoable, that is, changing the direction of government. It's not the work of a savior. It requires the hard, determined labor and compromise of many, many people. But they're getting things done.

To some, however, that's an unsatisfactory solution. They want a single heroic figure to descend from heaven and fix everything with a wave of his sword. Real life doesn't work that way. Will somebody please explain that to the Perot groupies? America doesn't need a demagogue. We don't need any more Huey Longs. *Most* of us don't, I should say. The rest cling to their belief in Perot, blind to his shortcomings, his warts, his failures.

What are these people *really* looking for? My own hunch is that they're trying to fill a void in their lives. Politicians have been experts at sensing that weakness and taking advantage of it. They say to people, "We can fill that emptiness. We will shower you with attention—and government programs." But no government, no matter how ingenious, no matter how capably run, can fill the emotional needs of human beings. No government can play the part of a strong, all-wise father or a warm, nurturing mother or a reliable friend, let alone a savior. When people look to politicians for love and security, they're in big trouble.

That's when charlatans—like Ross Perot—can exploit them.

# The Religious Right, the Pro-life Movement, and Other Zealots and Fanatics

———— ◆ ————

BEFORE I GET INTO THIS, I SHOULD STATE THAT IT'S NOT JUST THAT I'm uncomfortable with the religious right—I'd be uncomfortable with the religious left, if such a thing were imaginable. I don't like religion in politics. I'm not particularly religious, but if I were, you can bet that I'd keep it to myself. I don't like proselytizers. I don't like people who take whatever you say and twist it to suit their own religious beliefs. I'm not comfortable with people who try to inflict their religion on others.

In fact, some of the most intolerant people I've ever known professed to be religious. I know that there are many communities that are stable, solid, and crime-free because they do have religious cohesion. So it isn't religion that I'm against. It's the way religion is used by a lot of hypocrites. If a person or a family or a community has religious beliefs, that's all well and good. And if those religious beliefs determine how they feel about community standards, that's all right, too.

However, if the law protects somebody else's privacy and right to do something, even if your religion believes that it is abhorrent and evil, you must abide by the law.

Now, the first thing to keep in mind about the religious right is that it is no different from any other special-interest group that seeks to have undue influence over the political process. They may claim to speak for God, but they operate in the same way as the AFL-CIO, the Sidney Hillman Political Action Committee, the Liberal party, or even the Communist Party USA.

For years the Democrats have had to put up with special-interest groups, and now it's the Republicans' turn. They have to listen to Ralph Reed of the Christian Coalition, Jerry Falwell, Pat Robertson, and all the rest.

Of course, the parties don't *have* to listen, but then they'd be taking their chances with all the sane, nonideological Americans who go to the polling place every election. So they pander to these big blocs of votes. It's a dangerous game, but it's a game that the parties can't resist playing.

Why is it dangerous? Because the parties must try to get all the votes the group can deliver without being devoured by the group. In truth, many of the religious right's concerns and beliefs are very similar to my own. But I have never liked the concept of a one-issue campaign. I don't like one-issue candidates. I don't like one-issue voters. The religious right has one main obsession that drives it, and frankly, as an American and as a Republican, that scares me.

I'm terrified of the consequences of this obsession with abortion.

If you are convinced that abortion is murder and is morally reprehensible, then, of course, you're dedicated to eradicating it. But if you do *not* believe that abortion is murder, and if you believe that abortion is preferable to what happens to so many children who, once they are born, are abused, neglected, even murdered, then you have to part company with the so-called right-to-life mob.

Legally, whether you like *Roe v. Wade* or not, a woman has a constitutional right to an abortion in the first three months of her pregnancy. When somebody goes and shoots the doctor or the aide to the doctor or the receptionist, then that is an example of religious beliefs run amok.

I once lived in Woodbridge, New Jersey, not too far from an abortion clinic. And every Saturday, without fail—rain or shine, snow, driving wind, the most inclement weather you could imagine—there was a group of zealots standing outside, holding up placards, denouncing what was going on, even taunting the women going into the clinic. Eventually, even that method of protest was not enough. The place was firebombed and put out of business. Nobody died in that particular incident and nobody was injured, but women could no longer go there and had to go elsewhere or forgo abortion altogether. The people who did that, I am certain, would claim to be acting out of religious belief.

But I say they had no right. They broke the law. They committed arson, they endangered people's lives, and they made a legal activity impossible. These people were not caught, they were not punished, and yet the authorities knew, I believe, who they were.

I remember driving by and seeing their placards invoking the will of God, invoking the deity, invoking Jesus Christ— anything they could use in the name of religion. And yet they committed very unreligious, antireligious acts. That is the trouble with religion. People use it as an excuse for all manner of ungodly behavior. Religious zealotry has been the cause of more pain, more anguish, more sorrow in the history of civilization than perhaps any other allegiance.

I don't have a problem with abortion. I'm sick and tired of people equating an unborn fetus with a born person. There's no comparison.

When I see all the illegitimate births in America, when I see the burgeoning welfare rolls, I would hope that we would have enough sense to practice pregnancy prevention. But when contraception is not practiced and a woman seeks to have an abortion, then she should be able to have it.

You know, we talk about abortion as though it's only been around since 1973. But it is as old as mankind. And it wasn't too long ago that women were going to clandestine abortionists, quite often to people who really didn't have medical training, and were subjecting themselves to great risk in their attempts to have abortions.

Even in my mother's generation women knew about abortion. There was a story about an aunt who had taken laxatives, hot baths, jumped on trampolines—did everything under the sun to abort an unwanted pregnancy. People talked in hushed terms about how she tried to abort using all these different, useless methods.

So why do some people act as though it's never been thought of before? There are a lot of people who have told me, perhaps tongue in cheek, that it would have been okay with them if they had been aborted. Which sounds silly, because if you were aborted, you wouldn't know it! Jean-Paul Sartre asked this question: What is life but an unnecessary interruption to pleasant nonexistence? So why do we interrupt pleasant nonexistence? Why do we insist on it?

If we were really a mature society, of course, we wouldn't be in the predicament we're in. If we had honest leadership, if we weren't afraid of being called racist and other names, we would embark on what I call "the Bob Grant mandatory sterilization program."

This program occurred to me back in 1970, as the illegitimate birthrate began to rise. I began to notice that teenage girls or women in their early twenties were having four, five, six illegitimate children. And each time they would produce a child, they would get free prenatal care, natal care—the delivery, the obstetrics, all the ancillary amenities—and postnatal care, including a stipend, which would vary depending on where the mother lived.

And I thought *In heaven's name, since we are paying for all this, it makes us a party to it, so why don't we have any say in it?* If you're a responsible adult, you figure out how many children you can afford to raise before you have them. And here we are, supporting children we never chose to have! We are reduced to arguing about what to give the woman once she has had the baby. Which is a ridiculous argument, because once the baby is born, it's born. How could we turn our backs on a baby? There are those who say, "Well, don't give her any more money!" Okay, fine—but you're punishing the baby! That's when I thought: "Wouldn't it make much more sense to prevent that pregnancy?"

Now, some feminists have chastised me severely because I've talked about tubal ligation. There's two ways to do a tubal ligation: There's a tube cut, which renders the woman barren for the rest of her life. Not a bad idea. But you can also have a woman's tubes *tied,* meaning it can be undone if the woman's financial situation changes. This was before

Norplant, before temporary chemical sterilization was invented.

Well, these feminists came down on me—the Gloria Steinem crowd—and they said I was a misogynist and a typical chauvinist pig, because I put all the onus on the woman. And I said, "Well, I have no problem with vasectomies, but how do we find the studs who are creating these pregnancies? If we could find them and hold them down for the urologist, fine!" But you can't find them.

I recall interviewing a woman on a show on WMCA many years ago, and she defiantly told me that she didn't know who the fathers of her brood were. She was pretty sure about the father of her first child, but the other three had unclear origins. And she was only twenty-two years old. Instead of being somewhat contrite, she was pugnacious, hostile, in essence saying: "How dare you tell me what to do?!" There is an old saying—I know it's out of style—beggars can't be choosers. Well, these people are nothing more than beggars, and yet they're telling us what we have to do for them. They're ordering us; we've got everything turned inside out.

And it's a great pity, because the proliferation of illegitimates is the costliest problem in American society today. In and of itself it's costly, but then the subsequent cost is incalculable! Because these illegitimate creatures grow up to be the warriors, the stalkers, the marauders, the robbers, the rapists, the muggers—swelling the ranks of the predators out there.

Of course, sex education was supposed to save our society from the ravages of illegitimacy and poverty caused by people having more children than they could afford to support. Remember that, sex education? They've been teaching nothing but sex education since the 1960s! What have the schoolchildren learned, except how to put it in? It's totally absurd! They teach it like a mechanics class: the piston goes here, the cylinder goes there. No, the emphasis has to be on preventing pregnancies instead of, "Well, here's the penis, here's the vagina. The penis goes here . . ."

I recall when sex education really got rolling. I was on KABC in Los Angeles at the time, and in those days a lot of callers were very naive—they thought common sense would prevail. The educators should have been attempting to instill in young people the need for abstinence. They should have taught that you're monkeying around with something very profound and serious when you're having casual sex.

In olden days, we relied on women to have a sense of honor, a sense of morality, when it came to sex. Then women's lib came along, promising equality. And instead of men becoming more responsible, women became *less* so! Progress! Equality!

Maybe it's too late to imbue young people with sense in this realm of life. I think we ought to try to encourage abstinence as much as possible. I think we ought to make it less fashionable to be out getting laid at thirteen. But I realize that I'm swimming upstream here. I don't expect this book to stem the tide; I don't guess that many of my readers are responsible for the illegitimacy catastrophe. We're hell-bent on our own destruction; I'm telling you that if we do not do these things, we're doomed. We need more abortions, not fewer. We need birth control taught in a way that actually controls the number of births.

These are, I realize, fairly atypical views coming from a conservative. But who said I was a typical conservative? I have to laugh: people say, "Oh, this guy calls himself a conservative—therefore, he *has* to believe in the following." First we're labeled, and then we're expected to live up to the label. That kind of thinking reduces a human being to the level of a tin can. You can't see what's inside, but you label it anyway. You open it up and you find that it's a can of mixed vegetables: maybe it has corn, peas, carrots, string beans. And you're shocked. You say, "Well, I thought it was gonna be all string beans! It's gotta be all string beans!" Well, I'm *not* all string beans, and I think anybody who *is* so easily labeled is too doctrinaire and rigid to be really thinking about each issue. And I like to think that I take each issue on its own merits.

In fact, I think most people feel that way. I've come to the conclusion that Barbara Bush was absolutely correct in 1992 when she said that an abortion plank, either for or against, has no place in a political platform. I was in Houston for the Republican convention that infamous year, and I heard a lot of the grumbling, infighting, fraction, and tension that the pro-life plank was causing. Unfortunately, that kind of kow-towing to the religious right plays into the hands of the Democrats, because they exploit that division. And by doing that, they won the White House and will continue to pick up voters turned off by the religious radicals within the Republican party.

Now, what could be worse than that?

# *The Right to Control Arms*

———— ◆ ————

I DON'T LIKE GUNS. I'VE HAD MANY OPPORTUNITIES TO BRING A PIS-
tol into my home for self-defense and chose not to do so. I
know of too many people who were shot, and sometimes
killed, by guns in their own homes.

However, if my neighbor wants a gun, and he's willing to
get and use it in a lawful and sane way, I think he has a
right. In fact, I *know* he does—the Constitution makes it
pretty clear, and if we're going to live by that document, we
have to accept it one hundred percent.

Does that mean I'm in favor of gun control? Yes, it does.
For some reason, Americans get into more trouble with guns
than do people anywhere else. Our national murder and
armed robbery statistics are a disgrace. So it's clear—we must
have and enforce laws that regulate gun ownership and use.
We can't let just anybody own such a fierce weapon. We
must do our best to keep guns out of the wrong hands, and
we must punish severely people who break the laws.

People who want to own guns should have to prove themselves to be good citizens—law-abiding, mentally stable, responsible human beings—before they're licensed to own a
firearm. No felons should own guns. No loonies. And before
we allow anyone to buy a gun, he or she must learn to use it
safely and wisely, and then be able to prove that knowledge.

Now, the NRA and others will say, "Yeah, but what about the criminals? When guns are outlawed, only outlaws will have guns." And they're right. What we really need is *criminal control.* But until that happy day arrives, we must do our best to regulate gun crime. We can't stop the flow of cocaine and heroin into America, but we don't give up trying. And we have no problem with licensing drivers and automobiles, or with making sure that drivers actually know how to drive and can prove it. That doesn't eradicate all auto accidents, sure, but still we believe that caution and licensing make a difference.

I can accept that some people like to hunt, and they should have their rifles. I know that some people need handguns to defend themselves, and I certainly wouldn't deny them a fighting chance against the scum running wild in our streets. But I have no idea why anybody except a police officer needs an automatic or semiautomatic weapon. I am sure that nobody has a lawful need for armor-piercing bullets. So it's possible to regulate guns without banning them.

Aside from everything else, the issue of guns and gun control is a bane to anybody who does a talk radio show. No other subject engenders such fervent opinions. I'll never understand that passion, but I believe it is genuine. If so many normal Americans want guns, you can't take away that right without doing even more damage than you're trying to avoid.

# Slick Willie's Sick Game

—— ◆ ——

EVEN AS I'M WRITING THESE PAGES, THE INDIGNITIES THAT COME with having Slick Willie in the White House continue to pile up.

Do you require any further evidence of his complete and total inadequacy and ineptitude? He is the president of the United States, what used to be called the most powerful position in the entire world. We once had presidents who used that bully pulpit well, if not always wisely. They were true presidents; they didn't deign to snuffle and whimper and wrestle around in the mud with mere mortals. They understood the enormous power they possessed and wielded it as though they deserved nothing less. Publicly, at least, they carried themselves like true successors to George Washington, like vicars of democracy and freedom.

Like presidents!

Now we have to make do with a crybaby. We have to look up to a whiner who is on a constant, panicky search for a way to weasel out of the blame, a fat little boy who likes to point his pudgy finger and bleat about the baddies who are picking on him.

When the Republicans crushed the Democrats at the polls in November of 1994, Slick Willie needed to evade the message. He couldn't bear to hear this utter rejection of him, his wife, and everything he offered us.

So he blamed talk radio. In a way, he was absolutely right. Talk radio represents the democratization of the mass media. When the total domination of liberals in TV, radio, print, and cyberspace finally became too oppressive to bear, the great monolith toppled. What took its place is a healthy diversity of opinion at every level. Information, the force that had become more powerful than any statesman or political party, was finally liberated. That's why the Democrats were defeated—*all* sides of the truth can now actually be heard.

Nobody took Slick Willie's caterwauling seriously back then. It was more amusing than anything else.

Then, the hideous Oklahoma City bombers struck. Slick Willie sensed that beneath the madness and depredation, there was a message meant for him. Did he rise to the occasion like a true president and call on the American people to stand brave and firm against anarchy and terror and treason? No, he did not. It's not in him to stand brave and firm against anything.

Instead, he once again pointed his shaky little finger at talk radio.

Some subhuman vermin blew up a building and killed more than a hundred decent, innocent people, including children. And Slick Willie decided that talk radio deserved a share of the blame. Why? Because we're antigovernment? No, nothing could be further from the truth. All the conservative talk radio hosts I've ever heard profess nothing but *love* for America. We spend endless hours arguing about how our country can be made even greater than it is.

No, he's blaming us because we're anti-Clinton and anti-liberal policies. He thinks Americans will believe that to criticize him is to call for the destruction of the United States. How pathetic.

And then, when he was called on his lie—when people demanded to know exactly *which* radio shows he was referring to—he exposed his own spineless nature. He backed down. He said he had been misunderstood. What a disgusting spectacle, to watch our own president behave first like a weenie, then like a chicken.

People who call in to talk radio shows sometimes do say intemperate things. It goes with the territory. But they're not mad bombers. During Slick Willie's heyday, the sixties, the yippies and Panthers and the rest of the scum said intemperate things. Had Richard Nixon gone before the TV cameras and suggested that the Smothers Brothers were responsible for the Weathermen, we'd still hear the wails of protest. People should never confuse what talk-radio callers say with what the host believes. Any caller, at any time, can say anything. That's what democracy is all about.

The slime who blew up the federal building aren't conservatives—they're maniacs. Maniacs don't hold rational views. Maniacs don't work through the system. Maniacs don't bother discussing our national problems. And they don't take their cues from talk radio. I don't know what Slick Willie is smoking these days, but he should give his brain cells a break.

# The Silver-Haired Menace

———— ◆ ————

THE MOST EFFECTIVE PROPAGANDA MACHINE IN THE COUNTRY ISN'T the NRA or NOW or the GOP or any of the other usual suspects.

It's the AARP. The American Association of Retired People. That and the rest of the senior citizen lobby.

Old people today get away with murder. We've spoiled them with more benefits and special programs and discounts than any welfare fraud or farm-subsidy con artist could dream of. And still they want more.

The AARP has millions and millions of loyal members who will do anything their leadership tells them to. The AARP actually wants to dictate policy to the United States Congress, without any concern for the wage-earners and taxpayers who have to pick up the bills. Every politician is scared to death to even discuss Social Security or Medicare because of these old geezers. The federal, state, and local governments bend over backward to keep the oldsters happy, because every politician knows this simple fact: Old people vote.

They won't give up a nickel of what they're getting, even though in many instances they don't really need our help. Newt Gingrich and the 104th Congress are trying to *save* Medicare, and the AARP says, "How dare you try to do that at *our* expense?" No—they'd rather see it go bankrupt than have to be a little more careful about running up their medical tabs.

It truly is about to go broke, too. At the present level of spending, Medicare will be officially bankrupt in 2002, just six years from now. Even the fogies concede that waste and fraud are responsible for the mess we're in. But they won't stand for a sensible solution—namely, cutting back on funding, which would force the waste and fraud out of the system. They want to see the impossible happen: they want the waste and fraud to go away on their own, without the pressure of cuts. It'll never happen that way, of course, but they don't care. Most of them won't be around to see what life without Medicare is like.

These oldsters kill me. They actually believe that they're only getting back in Social Security and Medicare what they put into the system. In fact, people who turn sixty-five now will, on average, get back what they put in (plus interest) during their first seven years of retirement. After that, they're living off the money that *we're* paying in taxes. In all, on average, they'll get back four times as much as they paid in. It's welfare for old people, plain and simple—and they get it whether they need it or not. Even our so-called welfare system is more justifiable than this boondoggle.

I think we've pampered the old people. I think that they've become spoiled. They want their senior discounts for every purchase they make. They want to get on a bus, go to a show, shop a little, have dinner—all with ten percent off.

And yet, according to statistics, they have most of the money. Not the younger people. According to a study by Merrill Lynch, based on census figures, here's the breakdown of our nation's savings: People aged 65–74 lead the pack, with around $10,000 in the bank per household; those 75 and over have about $8,000; aged 55–64, close to $7,000; from 45–54, under $3,000, and people aged 35–44, *less than $1,000.*

The AARP, in case you don't know, was started back before Medicare as a health insurance company for retired teachers. Once Medicare made it redundant, some genius said, "Hey, I've got a great way for us to keep this business

going. We'll be lobbyists for old people and get them every
benefit we can think of. In fact, we'll even enroll nonretired
people, starting at age fifty, just to keep our numbers high.''

Is fifty old? No, but the AARP doesn't care. The increased
membership makes the threat of AARP displeasure that much
harsher. To the senior citizens out there, I say stop acting
like a bunch of spoiled brats. You've got to do your part to
save Medicare. Stop being so damn selfish.

# One Subject Even
# I'm Afraid Of

◆

I'M ABOUT TO DISCUSS WHAT IS PERHAPS THE TOUCHIEST SUBJECT IN
this entire book, which is really saying something. This is a
controversial topic that even *I* hate to treat honestly.

Recently, I had to take two actions with regard to my ninety-
one-year-old mother. First, I had to give surgeons permission
to perform an operation on her. And second, I had to put her
in a nursing home. If she had not had the operation, the doctors
told us, she would not have lived much longer. So even though
she didn't want any surgery, I signed the consent form. She
was very angry with me, but what else could I do?

She doesn't like her life much these days. She misses her
own home; she's an independent-minded woman who liked to
cook and sew. But she could no longer continue on her own.

So I put her in the nursing home. Even at her age and in
her condition, she is one of the more able-bodied people in
that place. She's alert, she talks and attempts to read, although her cataracts get in the way (she refuses to have *that*
operation, and I won't force her).

But the other people in the home are pretty bad off—im-
prisoned in wheelchairs, mouths hanging open, drooling,
gazing endlessly at the ceiling or into space. Of course, it
takes a lot of money to keep them in there. Is that humane?

Believe me, I spend a lot of time wondering. Maybe in a

brave new world of tomorrow we will adopt a form of euthanasia that will spare us the needless prolongation of existence, which cannot be enjoyable to these people. Such a decision would also ease the tremendous burden on Medicare and taxpayers. The average person spends ninety percent of all the money he'll *ever* spend on medical bills in the last two years of his life. To what end? What is the goal? So that there'll be a different number on the tombstone? So that instead of saying 1996, it's 1997 or 1998?

Richard Lamm, the former Democratic governor of Colorado, is a rare politician; he actually speaks honestly. He once talked about the futility, and the cruelty, of keeping old people breathing. Notice I don't say keeping old people *living*. Because you can't call their existence a life. We can, however, keep them breathing. Vegetating.

Now, of course, there are people who remain spry and lively even at one hundred. Just as there are others who become senile and helpless in their sixties. What kind of society are we that we pretend we can't tell the difference? What kind of people insist on prolonging bodily functions just to pretend we are sustaining life? Do we really think we're doing these poor elderly souls a favor? Or is it ourselves whom we're placating?

Now, you might say, "Well, where there's life there's hope." But that has nothing to do with an old man or woman hanging on the precipice of death. We insist on using euphemisms whenever age and mortality are being discussed. Like "senior citizen." They're old people. Or "convalescent home." Look up the word "convalescence"—it has to do with recovery.

Who recovers from old age?

# Propaganda,
# Special Interests,
# and Business as Usual

◆

NOT LONG AGO, A FAN OF THE SHOW SENT ME A VERY HANDSOME
.45-caliber air pistol. It only shot BBs, but it was a strikingly
realistic creation, a nice piece of work.

He sent it because I was complaining on the air about
squirrels running all around my property, eating the wires
in my car's engine. But I never even used the gun. In fact, I
never took it out of the box. As I've said many times, I'm
not a big fan of guns, of any kind.

Then, lo and behold, the fan began contacting me, telling
me that I should change my pro–gun control stand. He made
it clear how much he disagreed with remarks I had made on
the subject.

I realized then, this man felt that because he had sent me
a gift, I owed him something in return. He thought that giving
me a toy gun meant I was obligated to change my opinion
on an important matter.

I sent the gun back right away. To hell with him.

That's just human nature, though, isn't it? You give gifts
to people you love and like because your feelings move you
to do so. But beyond that, you give to get something in return. A salesman gives presents to a client to ensure future
business. A peasant gives gifts to a king to guarantee favor-
able treatment.

And then there are campaign contributors and PACs and lobbyists.

Do the rules of normal human conduct and expectations apply in this realm? Elected officials and corporations depend on our willingness to pretend that they do not. But of course, they do.

Consider the friendly, civic-minded sugar industry. Do you know what a pound of sugar would cost if the free market were allowed to set its price? Maybe a dime. Why are you paying more than that? Because our laws keep out imported sugar and limit the use of beet sugar. The laws all but force us to buy sugar that comes from Louisiana or Hawaii.

Why do the lawmakers care so much about sugar? Because the major sugar companies see to it that they do, thanks to lobbyists and campaign contributions. You won't live long enough to see a senator from Louisiana vote to allow more imported sugar into this country.

Let's not single out sugar, though. Let's think about milk for a second. The dairy industry exposed itself in the 1972 election between George McGovern and President Richard Nixon thusly: It contributed $10,000 to *both* candidates.

Now, was the dairy industry just confused? Was this simply a case of indecision over the policies of two dramatically different candidates? Or do dairy tycoons just believe in the right of every candidate to run a well-financed race?

Get real—they didn't care *who* won. They probably preferred Nixon and saw that McGovern was a long shot. But, they figured, we want whoever wins to be our pal in the White House. It was a totally cynical, practical decision to guarantee the future of dairy price supports. You don't *have* to care who becomes president if you have the money to influence any winner into doing your bidding. The only philosophy you have to put your faith in is the one that says, "Money talks."

What's important to remember in all this is that Congress and the president can't really give anything away, not tax breaks or price subsidies or anything else. They don't have it to give—until they take it from *us*. That $20,000 the dairy trade contributed to Nixon and McGovern was but a pittance compared to the fortune the government puts back into the dairy tycoons' pockets. And that fortune comes out of what you pay in taxes. If somebody gets a tax abatement, the government doesn't automatically spend less money—it just takes more from you and me.

Many years ago, when I was interviewing a United States senator, I asked him about lobbyists. In those days, mind you, "lobbyist" wasn't a bad word yet.

And he said, "Oh we're very grateful to the lobbyists, because they help educate us. They keep us informed." Now, think about that a second. Our legislators are getting their information on important issues from lobbyists. That means lawmakers are spoon-fed slanted, self-serving, deceptive propaganda. And they think it's information. It's scary, when you think of all these lobbyists wining and dining our lawmakers and filling their heads with half-truths, quarter-truths, near-truths, and other garbage.

It's a crooked, corrupt, absurdly dishonest way to run a country. But nobody with the power to change it will do so, because that would jeopardize their high-priced campaigns.

So how do we solve it? I don't know if we can. The focus of late has been on reining in the lobbyists, but that's foolish, I think. They should be allowed to speak and present their views. It's not *their* fault the politicians pay attention to them. Our officials could listen to the lobbyists and then decide to do what's best for the taxpayers, instead of what the sugar lobby or the dairy lobby or the tobacco lobby or the gun lobby or the senior citizen lobby wants.

But they won't do that until we force them to. In the absence of a "normal Americans" lobby, we have to use our votes to make the politicians listen to us. One informed, educated voter can't make a real difference. A nation of them could. This is *our* problem to solve, not the politicians'.

# One Bad Conservative Cause

———— ◆ ————

BEING A CONSERVATIVE, I'M SUPPOSED TO BE FOUR-SQUARE FOR term limits. I can even think of many good arguments for them. And yet, there's something deep inside me that is against term limits.

Maybe it's my pragmatic side that says, look, if someone's doing a good job and has gained experience and savvy, why prohibit him from continuing to do it? We don't run businesses that way.

Then, there's also the issue of freedom of choice. If we say voters can choose their representatives, why disqualify someone they obviously like?

It's true that we already have term limits where the presidency is concerned—two terms and you're out. But maybe that principle is wrong. Maybe we should be free to elect whomever we want.

It's easy to have term limits without passing any legislation. When you think an official has reached his limit, vote him out of office. Make an issue of it, just like taxes and abortion and everything else we consider at election time.

But let's not legislate yet another solution to a dubious problem. Even though term limits are a conservative cause, they're a big-government approach. They seem to say, "Normal people can't be entrusted with this responsibility, so we'll pass a law. We'll save them the trouble of thinking and acting for themselves." If conservatives truly are trying to end government interference in the lives of Americans, they'll find something worthier to do than "protecting" us from ourselves.

# *Our Deadbeat Nation*

———— ◆ ————

FOR A LONG TIME, WE EVADED FISCAL RESPONSIBILITY BY HAVING A government that went into the hole to make ends meet. But if we don't get a balanced budget soon, the whole house of cards will collapse. *You* couldn't borrow money indefinitely, without ever worrying about how you'd pay it back. At some point, the interest alone would crush you. The same principle works for our nation.

Now, does that mean you'd never go into debt? No. If you lost your job and had no cash coming in, debt would become unavoidable. Similarly, if, say, you suffered some uninsured disaster—the roof on your house blew off or the foundation cracked—you'd borrow if you had to, without blinking an eye.

Similarly, there are only two times in the life of a nation when an unbalanced budget can be justified. During the Depression, we went into the hole, and that was necessary. If another one comes along, we'd do the same again. And in wartime, of course, you can't worry about the deficit. When the very life of the country is at stake, you spend what you must in order to save it.

Other than during those crises, however, it's unconscionable to run up a national debt. It would be as if during the normal course of events, your own spending became greater than your earnings. You'd have no choice but to cut back on something. We have no choice either.

The national debt got so high and the budgets became so unbalanced because of politicians who pander for votes. They responded to every problem with a program, and most people cheered. Citizens never stopped to consider that they'd be the ones paying for those programs. Deficit spending was a way to put off the day of reckoning, but that day always comes in the end. If we had been made to pay in full for those programs, instead of creating unbalanced budgets, our tax obligations would have been even higher than they are today. Imagine that.

But we would have been better off that way. Instead, we're paying for the programs *and* for the interest on what we borrowed. By now, the politicians who created those programs are either dead or retired, so they don't care. They left this mess for us.

# *Mario, Ed, and Rudy*

$\blacklozenge$

NEW YORK HAS ALWAYS HAD MORE THAN ITS SHARE OF POLITICIANS who gain the national spotlight. It's not that our elected officials are any better than those from other places. They just stand out, for better or worse (usually the latter).

I first met Mario Cuomo during the Forest Hills crisis, when New York Mayor John Lindsay wanted to build low-income high-rise housing and there was a hue and cry against it by the residents of Queens. Lindsay appointed Cuomo to be the arbitrator, in hopes he could work out an agreement. Cuomo called me and said, "We've never met, but my wife's brother says I could learn a lot from you." Mario was a funny guy. He said, "I don't want my in-laws mad at me, so I'm calling."

We had lunch at an Italian restaurant in Manhattan, just the two of us, and he said, "Look, I want to pick your brain. You're popular, and you talk to people all the time on your show." And that's how the relationship started—very cordially.

We had a lot in common because of our Italian background and our interest in politics. But we didn't discuss that subject at our first meeting, because I had sized Mario up as an old-time, entrenched New Dealer. And I knew we wouldn't find much to agree on.

Still, I liked him. I admired his intelligence, his erudition, his sense of humor—a very charming guy. As matter of fact, if it weren't for politics, I would have liked to have been his friend. If I think a politician's views are not good for my state or my city or my country, I'll oppose him whether I like him or not. So even though I liked Mario and got a kick out of him, I could not support him.

And he knew that. But we didn't let it get in the way. In 1977, when he lost the election for mayor of New York, he spent an incredible two hours on the air with me, in which he unloaded a lot of his real feelings about the experience. I remember one of the things he said was, "Now it's your turn, Bob." As though he wasn't going to do it ever again. And I think that on that particular night he really felt like he didn't want to run for office anymore. The experience left him tired and disappointed. So even then he was waffling about his future in the public arena.

Then, during the presidential campaign of 1980, Lieutenant Governor Mario Cuomo was about the only prominent Democrat in the state who came out strongly for Jimmy Carter. The others liked Kennedy or hedged their bets by backing no one in particular. But Cuomo was the point man for Carter, and he campaigned faithfully. Even though it looked like a losing cause, he never stopped campaigning. He was a good soldier for the Democrats. And I remember his being on my show shortly before the 1980 election, confessing that even his own father was going to vote for Ronald Reagan.

Two years later, of course, Mario ran for governor and he won. And I had him on my show, along with Ed Koch, for several debates. So while we never agreed on important political matters, we always had respectful lines of communication.

That began to change when he ran for his second term as governor, against Andy O'Rourke, Westchester County county executive. I felt it was a very unfair campaign: Cuomo had all the money and all the support; O'Rourke had neither. And still Cuomo was raising more, and all the editorial writers around town were questioning his war chest, wondering what all that money was needed for.

Now, Mario was certainly not going to put it in his back

pocket. He may be a lot of things, but he's an honest man. I believed at the time that the war chest was there to prepare him for a 1988 presidential run. Everybody else seemed to believe that, too.

I had him on my show—I think it was Halloween, 1986—and I asked him several times about the war chest. "Andy O'Rourke doesn't even have one million; you have eight million. Why do you need all that money?" But he wouldn't give me a straight answer on that, so I brought it up again and again. Finally, his Neapolitan temper got the better of him, and he hung up on me. He said, "Is that all? If that's all you have to ask about, good-bye!" And we have never talked since.

Did I mention that he's a touchy guy?

I shouldn't have been surprised about that. I once saw him wrestle—seriously scuffle—with Mike Long, the chairman of the Conservative party of New York, during a mayoral campaign. I saw them bouncing each other off the wall. It started when Mike said something to a reporter that got into the paper, and Mario didn't like it and started giving Mike hell and poking his finger in Mike's face. So Mike says, "Hey, don't you poke your finger at me!" And the next thing you know, they're going at it. For real. So I knew that Mario's the kind of guy who takes everything to heart.

We became sworn enemies during his last campaign. I started doing shtick about him, just kidding around. And it got me thinking of those old-time Italian guys I heard when I was a boy, and something they'd always say came into my head: *"Hey, tu sei un proprio sfaccim."* Which means, "You're a real lowlife." The first person I ever heard say that was my grandma Teresa, my mother's mother. She got mad at somebody—as a matter of fact, it was Franklin D. Roosevelt. She used to *love* FDR. Then, I don't know what the heck happened, but in 1940 or 1941, she changed her mind. And I heard her call him *"un proprio sfaccim."* I got such a kick out of that word. I don't know why, but it cracks me up. It's just a silly word! And on the air that day, I was being silly.

But it stuck. People liked it, and that's how the *sfaccim* T-shirts came about, and I started going back to it. I said,

"Every state has a governor except New York. We're privileged—we have a *sfaccim.*" Other people can say far worse things—Howard Stern or Don Imus come to mind—and listeners say, "Oh, how funny they are." I say something fairly mild, and it's taken so seriously. No matter how silly I get, people take me seriously. It's either a blessing a curse, depending on how you want to look at it.

The professional Italians didn't like it at all. They were very upset about it and wrote letters. They felt it was demeaning, that it was a slur against Italians. You know, people will complain no matter what.

Then I heard, through a third party—meaning that I don't know if it's true and have no way of finding out—that Mario Cuomo's wife, Matilda, was very upset and hurt about it. She and I had once been fond of each other, but she told somebody who wanted to interview her that she wouldn't discuss me at all because she and Mario were too hurt by my behavior. I had also heard that she told Mario, "Why don't you say something to that guy?" And he said he didn't want to give me the satisfaction. He said, "That's what that son of a bitch wants—he wants to arouse my ire, he wants me to respond, and it's killing him that I don't, so I'm not going to say a word. I'm not going to lower myself."

Former mayor (and current radio talk-show host) Ed Koch is a likable guy, a born showman, and a born politician for at least one reason—he makes sure he covers his ass all the time. Maybe I could learn a lesson from him. Whenever he says something—and he does have the ability to tell it like it is—he's always careful to protect himself from retaliation by his enemies. For instance, when I would criticize Jesse Jackson for calling New York "Hymietown," I would attack him and leave it at that. Whenever Ed Koch criticizes a black, he always reminds his audience that he has also criticized Meir Kahane and David Duke. He makes sure his listeners know he has criticized *everybody* for doing or saying evil. We all know by now that Ed Koch is not a bigot. And I really think he ought to cut the equivocating out. But he was elected mayor of New York City three times, so who am I to argue with the guy?

I have a photo in my desk that shows me holding an umbrella over Ed Koch and myself at the Bronx County Columbus Day Parade in 1977, the same year he ran for mayor. I was grand marshal of the parade that year. Ed Koch had a well-known gimmick of always asking people, "How'm I doing?" And he came over to me at the parade and asked his favorite question, and I said, "You're doing very well." He asked, "Do you think I'll win?" And I said, "Yes, I do." He was a little concerned about the fact that he did not have the Liberal party endorsement and Mario Cuomo did, and he thought that maybe Mario Cuomo might beat him.

Now, in 1977 Ed Koch was my choice for mayor of New York. He was for the death penalty and sounded more conservative than Cuomo, so he was my man. But one Sunday in September, *The New York Times* had a front-page story that named Mario Cuomo's advisers. The reporter asked Cuomo whom he listened to, and he said, "Well, I take advice from a lot of people: Bob Grant and Pete Hamill and Jimmy Breslin . . ." That was a fair comment, but in the article it made it seem as though I was practically in his kitchen cabinet.

David Garth, who was managing the Koch campaign, had a fit. He said it was unfair that a Cuomo supporter was doing three or four hours of radio every day. Koch's lawyers actually came up to the station and listened to tapes—hours and hours of my show—to try and prove that the station owed them equal time.

Well, after they were through, one of the attorneys monitoring the tapes said that it sounded like I was for Koch, not Cuomo. Another one said he really couldn't tell whom I wanted. The truth was that while I liked Mario personally back then, I couldn't vote for him.

In the beginning of Koch's first term as mayor, when he was asked about diversity in his cabinet, he said that if he happened to pick twelve red-haired, green-eyed Irishmen, it would be because they're the best people for the job. In other words, he wasn't going to select people on the basis of ethnicity, race, or gender—he just wanted the best people. He took a lot of heat for that, but during his first term and part of the second term, he was very determined.

Then, the racial activists started to get to him, to wear him down, and he began to compromise. Perhaps wisely, from his perspective. But although he was a completely honest man, he ended up surrounded by corruption. Maybe that was the price of all his compromises. What I objected to was when he began to sound arrogant—that's why I started calling him "The Emperor." He took for granted that he would have five terms in office. By the end, though, people tired of him.

I first met our current mayor, Rudy Giuliani, in the 1980s, when he was still the U.S. attorney here. My friend U.S. Marshal Romolo Imundi said, "Bob, you've got to meet Rudy. He's your kind of guy."

When we finally got together, Romolo said, kidding around, "Rudy, if you ever want to go into politics, this is the guy you've got to talk to."

And Rudy just smiled in that cryptic way of his. He's always had the ability to play his cards close to the vest. He and I talked on several occasions. Once, I heard from an inmate at the federal pen at Fishkill who claimed to have some juicy information about Mario Cuomo, and I asked Rudy if he could get me in to visit the guy. He made the phone calls and got me inside, though it turned out to be a wild goose chase. I would have swum the Hudson to learn something negative about Cuomo.

After Rudy announced for mayor in 1989, I probably made more campaign appearances with him than anybody else did. I introduced him to lots of Jewish groups in particular, because I have so many fans in Borough Park, Williamsburg, and Crown Heights.

Well, he made it into Gracie Mansion in 1994, and he's doing an excellent job, too. He's doing something that very few politicians do: he's trying to keep his campaign promises. It's an almost impossible job, because he is following on the heels of decades and decades of mayors, with the possible exception of Ed Koch, who did nothing but give in to unions, give in to pressure groups, give in to minority groups. Even Ed Koch didn't play as tough as Rudy does.

The biggest challenge has been regarding tax rates and the budget. New York's already got the highest rate of taxation in the country, so he couldn't raise them any more. Not without alienating his backers and driving businesses out of the city. We've already got too big a ratio of welfare recipients to taxpayers. So he had to cut the budget, cut waste, and then, through attrition, cut a lot of jobs.

If you think it's hard to do that at the federal level, I assure you that it's even harder here in New York. People expected him to fold once in office, but he's showing no sign. He's standing his ground regardless of who screams.

He is the right mayor at the right time. He has the stamina and the character that is needed for the job. He proved himself when he went ahead and unified the New York Police Department. It never made sense that we had separate departments for the city itself, for the transit system, and for public housing. Ed Koch talked about unifying them, but the pressure scared him away. Rudy didn't make a big deal of it— he just did it. He presented his case firmly and logically, and he stuck to his guns.

Rudy isn't always right, not in my opinion. He endorsed Mario Cuomo for governor against his own party's choice, George Pataki. Rudy made that dumb choice for one reason: He and Pataki's backer Senator Al D'Amato can't stand each other. Those two will never heal the wounds now. There's just too much deep resentment. I know this because I talk to both of them, and each complains to me about the other. Never publicly, though. They won't even admit there's a rift. Rudy especially is very shrewd that way.

I also didn't like it when he traveled all the way to Minnesota to appear with Slick Willie in support of the so-called crime bill. It was needless. If he wanted to back the bill, he could have done so long-distance. Instead, he allowed himself to stand on a platform with a terrible Democratic president. Why did he do it? To aggravate guys like me? Because he really thinks that it's important to show his support?

I think there's a third reason. He's thinking ahead. He's thinking, perhaps, about the day he'll run for higher office and might need the goodwill of Democratic and independent voters.

I know this—Rudy is incapable of making a move without having first thought it all the way through. He doesn't pull a risky stunt without having a very good reason.

# The World According to Grant

———— ◆ ————

THERE'S ONLY ONE AMERICA, OF COURSE, BUT THAT DOESN'T MEAN there aren't other countries I admire. And it follows that if I admire some foreign countries, there are others I despise.

My favorite foreign country? That's easy—Australia. Because the people there are civilized, gentle, decent, and law-abiding. You don't see graffiti. You don't see debris on the sidewalk. The people of Sydney actually *love* their city, and they treat it that way. You don't see that kind of civic sentiment many places.

I like New Zealand for the same reasons. Whether New Zealanders and Australians like to be compared or not is a different story, but to me they are very similar.

I had a good time in Singapore, because I wasn't creating graffiti, I wasn't throwing trash on the grass, I wasn't violating the law. I think Singapore is a magnificently safe and clean country. I don't want to live there, but I think they could teach us a lot about what to do with our perpetrators of crime and nuisance.

I admire Israel enormously. That country endures only because its people refused to surrender, refused to be frightened into nothingness. From the day Israel was created, the Arab League declared war on it, and Jordan and Egypt and Syria—to name just a few—all took that declaration seriously. And many people in this country said, "Well, Israel is so outnumbered, how can it last?" But Israel lasted and even prevailed. In 1948 and then in 1956 and then in 1967 and on October 3, 1973, the day of the Yom Kippur sneak attack, Israel was victorious. Israel can set a great example for any country that has to fight to be free and safe.

The country I *hate* most right now is Iraq, and I can tell you why in two words: Saddam Hussein. I still cannot reconcile that the same George Bush who was so brilliant in structuring the coalition that threw Iraq out of Kuwait, who showed such mastery of diplomacy and warfare, then let Hussein off the hook. George Bush vanquished that evil bastard, but then refused to finish him off. Iraq is a rogue nation, one that seeks the destruction of our ally, Israel. As long as Saddam Hussein lives, it will continue to represent a great threat to world peace, to stabilization in the Gulf, and to the state of Israel.

I hate Iran just about as much. I feel that we have never really gotten the revenge we deserve for the taking of our embassy there and the holding of the hostages. We have never really made them pay for what they did. I feel about Iran the way I feel about any criminal who gets off unpunished.

For many years I closed my program by saying: "Get Gadhafi." Some people wondered, "What the heck is he saying?" One woman said she thought I was saying, "Get me coffee!" I began signing off with that phrase after returning from my first trip to Israel, in 1971. There, I talked to Sergeant Albert Maya, a former member of the IDF—the Israeli Defense Force—and he told me that the Libyan dictator Muammar Gadhafi was behind most of the terrorist acts aimed at Israelis, but also at anybody who entered an airport in Rome, Athens, or anyplace else. I came home from that trip firm in my belief that as long as Gadhafi lives, he represents a grave threat to us all.

I stopped saying "Get Gadhafi" in 1986, when Ronald Reagan sent those F-11s that bombed Tripoli to bits, forcing Gadhafi to lower his posture for a spell. Now it appears that he was responsible for the sabotage of Pan Am flight 103.

So you can put Libya on my hate list, at least as long as Gadhafi lives.

You see, most often it isn't countries themselves that are bad, it's the people running them. For a long time Iran was an ally of ours, the linchpin of stability in the Middle East, because of the Shah. And then came the obsession to overthrow the Shah, brought about by Islamic fundamentalists and anti-American swine in this country. Yes, they got rid of the Shah. And we got his friendly replacement—the Ayatollah. What an improvement.

I certainly don't hate France, but I'm not too fond of it, either. The French are a very feckless people, an unreliable ally in many cases, and they seem to have an exalted opinion of themselves.

Finally, I think Canada's a joke. Quebec wants to be French? Let them. Then the rest of Canada can join the United States. That would make sense. Canada should be doing better than it is. It's rich in natural resources, and it enjoys a hearty, intelligent, and educated society. But because it allowed itself to be riven by the Quebec problem and because it embraced socialism, it is not doing well at all. As dire as I sometimes think things are here, I know we could show the Canadians a thing or two.

# Downward Mobility
## and the Kennedys

———— ◆ ————

I DIDN'T VOTE FOR JOHN F. KENNEDY, SO DON'T GET CARRIED AWAY
by what I'm about to say. But I did like him. He had a
charm about him. He had the ability to laugh at himself.
He didn't seem to take himself too seriously. And I think
that's why he was perceived as the winner in the famous
debate, because Richard Nixon was so grim and determined. Kennedy seemed to say, "Hey, if I win, I win, and
if I don't, so what?" I liked that insouciant quality about
him.

Even as a politician, I admired him, though as president
he promoted a lot of liberalism's worst programs. His one
and only inaugural speech, in 1961, was a *very* tough warrior
statement. "We will stand by any friend, we will oppose any
foe, in the cause of freedom." It was a message to the Soviet
Union that he was going to continue the policies of Harry
Truman and Dwight Eisenhower. His other famed sentiment—"Ask not what your country can do for you, ask what
you can do for your country"—is stirring, patriotic wisdom
that, sadly, was disregarded by his fellow Democrats, who
encouraged people to ask only what their country could do
for them.

So JFK was not without his strengths. And, yet, I would
never have voted for him. I am capable of liking a politician

182

without wanting him in office. I liked Adlai Stevenson, too. He was a good man. But I voted against him *twice.*

I didn't like Bobby Kennedy at all, because on top of being a liberal, he was an obvious opportunist. In 1967 he refrained from throwing his hat into the ring until after Gene McCarthy confronted his party's incumbent president head-on in the New Hampshire primary and did so well against Lyndon Johnson.

Only then did Bobby Kennedy say, *"Ohhh,* look what McCarthy did. I bet I could do even better." McCarthy would have won the California primary, no question, had Kennedy not entered the race. Bobby came out on top, only to lose his life before that day ended. But I won't be a hypocrite: I thought it was sleazy of Kennedy to do what he did to McCarthy.

The last and least of the Kennedy line, of course, is little Teddy. He never would have gotten close to the Senate if he weren't Bobby and John's brother. And he's been the biggest, phoniest knee-jerk liberal from the moment he entered Congress, right up to the present. But I hate him so much because I hate anybody who gets away with "murder."

Only a Kennedy would have had the power to seal the testimony from the inquest into Mary Jo Kopechne's slaying. And that's what it was, to my mind. You know, the lowly swimming pool mechanic who allegedly screwed up installing a vent has been criminally charged in the death of tennis star Vitas Gerulaitis. What Kennedy did on that infamous night in 1969 was far worse than what that bumbling tradesman did.

Kennedy was such a lowlife that after he got bombed, drove off the bridge, and abandoned his dying mistress, all he could think about was his own untarnished image. What a weakling. He actually tried to get his cousin to say that *he* was driving the car. This family-loving Kennedy said to his own relative, "You have nothing to lose. This could hurt my political career."

That alone should have been enough to end all respect for Kennedy. Instead, the idiotic people of Massachusetts keep sending him back to Washington to do to all of us what he did to poor Mary Jo. Maybe the voters feel responsible for what happened to John and Bobby. Maybe it's because the Republican party in that state is in shambles. But there's a good Republican governor there now, Bill Weld, and perhaps Teddy's days in office are numbered. Let's hope so. As they say, he's no John Kennedy.

# Ten Liberals Worth
# Keeping Around

—— ◆ ——

1.

2.

3.

4.

5.

6.

7.

8.

9.

10.

# I Love/Hate New York

◆

WHEN PEOPLE ASK, "BOB, HOW DID YOU BECOME SUCH AN ANGRY kind of radio host?" I have a short answer for them: New York did this to me.

In 1970, I was living in Los Angeles and loving it. I loved the climate. I loved the lifestyle. My children lived there. I had divorced their mother, but the kids and I saw each other all the time. It beat the hell out of Chicago.

But by then, my employer, Metromedia, had gotten out of the talk-radio business. And things looked pretty dry out there, jobwise, for me. So when I got a call from an executive with WMCA in New York, asking if I'd come east to meet him, of course I said yes.

The meeting went well. He told me how much his station wanted and needed someone like me and how they all held me in such high esteem and that they knew my reputation as the best talk host in the country, *blah blah blah*.

But my introduction to the city itself was something else. I hated New York at first sight. I had been here only once before, for a single day in 1952, back when the city was still somewhat civilized, and I didn't like it then, either. I didn't like the congestion or the dirt or the hurly-burly or the noise of the subways or the weather or anything else. And so I told him that while the offer was attractive, the idea of living here was not, and so I wasn't going to take it.

Then, as we were saying good-bye, this executive said something that stuck in me like a needle. He said, "Well, Bob—you know, it's just too bad that the number-one talk-show host in America doesn't want to come to the number-one market in America." And with that, he hooked me. It haunted me all the way back to California.

We continued to talk once I returned home, and finally he wore me down. I said they'd have to provide me with a dozen paid trips to California a year for me to take the job. He offered six and said they'd put me up at the hotel of my choice. That cinched it.

On September 12, 1970, I flew to New York, hating the city but enjoying the excitement of starting at a station that was about to go all talk for the first time.

I lived for a spell at a Sheraton on West 42nd Street, near Times Square. The hotel was fine, but the area was absolutely dreadful, and I despised it. It was even worse than it is today: seedy, run-down, and populated mostly by sleazy porn shops, hookers, and panhandlers. I was amazed at the audacity of the whores and the beggars. Eventually, I couldn't take it any longer, so I moved to Queens, which was a good compromise but still not sunny California. And *definitely* not home. I felt so out of place in New York that I told all my California friends, "Listen. I have a two-year contract, and the minute it's up I'll be back." I really believed that, too. That's why I didn't buy any property here when I moved. I said, "Why should I get comfortable? I'm going back to California."

Six weeks after I started my new job, I got a call from a fellow named Dave Crane, who had been the news director at the station I worked at when I left Los Angeles. Dave had taken a job as program director of a station in San Francisco, and he said, "Hey, Bob, we'd love to have you here. When can you join us?" And I said, "Dave—I'm *dying* to come back to California. I hate this city. I miss my kids. I'm homesick twenty-four hours a day."

But then I remembered that I had just signed a two-year contract. And that my new bosses had paid to move me and my car here. So I said, "Dave, I'd love to come. But I just don't think I can walk out on a contract." And he said he understood, but if anything happened, he'd love to hire me.

Well, from that moment on, something interesting began to occur. I think that subconsciously I wanted to get fired so I could head for the West Coast. Because suddenly, I was becoming irascible on the air. Argumentative. Feisty. Impatient with the callers and everyone else. I didn't care what anybody thought about me or my manners. I hated everything about New York, including my listeners. It wasn't any act, either. I was telling people off left and right, even worse than today.

One day a caller actually said, "Does the manager of your radio station know the way you talk to the public?" I replied, "I presume they're able to listen, the same as you do. I would imagine they have speakers in their offices. But I don't *care!* Let them *fire* me!"

I was asking for it all right. And naturally, here's what happened: The ratings came out and showed that I was the only guy at that station who had any decent numbers. Outside of the Barry Gray show at night, the rest of the talk hosts were just not making it.

I was catching on because, for the first time, a great many people in this city heard a man they could identify with politically. In those days, meaning 1970, *nobody* dared to be a public conservative. (Except, of course, for the great and brilliant William F. Buckley, who has always had the courage and the bankroll to make his own rules.) Back then, liberalism was chic. Hell, as the great journalist Tom Wolfe showed, even *radicalism* was chic. And because most Americans are politically naive, they went along like good little sheep with whatever seemed to be in style. Every hot movie star, scrawny rock singer, Kennedy-haired hack politician, chardonnay-liberal publishing executive, and Ivy League bookworm was spouting the predictable left-wing platitudes. And so most people, being idiots, were mouthing the clichés that their idols had adopted. People wore beliefs in the same way they wore bell-bottoms, sideburns, and sandals. As fashion statements.

And here I was, an unabashed conservative, mad as hell

and not going to take it anymore, and people began to identify with me. New Yorkers who felt silly wearing that year's
trendy beliefs started tuning in. "Hey!" they said, "this guy's
saying what I think!" And I was saying it the way they
wanted it said—un-mellow, un-groovy, un-let-it-all-hang-out.
They had no idea how much of my anger was simply about
having to spend even one more day in New York. They just
knew they liked it.

Not only were they listening on the radio, but soon they
began inviting me out so they could hear it in person. For
some reason, most of my early personal appearances were at
synagogues. One day a caller even asked, "Hey, what are you
doing going to all those synagogues?" I said, "They're the
ones who *invite* me! If a Catholic church calls, I'll go there,
too."

Part of the reason synagogues liked me was that on the air
I was a staunch ally of Israel. But after I would speak, people
would approach me and say, "You know, Bob, even though
we're registered Democrats, we agree with lots of the things
you think." It was a little surprising, because Jews have the
reputation of being true-blue liberals. But people would say,
"Bob, you remind me of my brother or my father-in-law or
my uncle." And that is quite a compliment, because it means
that people will gladly invite you (and your show) into their
homes. It means people see you as a member of the family.
And for any kind of broadcaster, radio or TV, that's the secret
of success.

So the irony was that the more I expressed my unhappiness about finding myself in New York, the more New York
embraced me. And the slimmer became my chances of ever
getting out of this city.

One day back then, the station's owner, Peter Straus, came
up to me and said, "You know, Bob, you're arguing with the
callers too much. You should *listen* to them." As a matter of
fact, the station was running a newspaper ad at the time
showing a telephone off the hook and the words "WMCA
Listens."

"Well, Peter," I said, "if you just want somebody to answer
the phone and listen to callers, you don't need me. Why
don't I just go back to California?" By then, of course, he

couldn't let me leave. So when my two years were up, he offered me a new contract with a fifty percent raise. And, lo and behold, in spite of everything, I was getting used to living in New York.

And along the way I also realized that I belong in New York and nowhere else. Because even the biggest klutz in New York has more sophistication than the average caller from other places. Even L.A. The New York listener is better informed. He may sound crude sometimes, but he has more awareness, more worldliness, than the typical caller from anywhere else.

One day, in fact, our City Hall reporter, a lifelong New Yorker named Danny Meenan, said to me, "You know what, Bob—you're New *Yawk*." At the time, I didn't know whether to be insulted or flattered. Now I guess I agree with him.

# IV
# Reflections in a Cracked Mirror

———— ◆ ————

*Are you as screwed up as the major media make you out to be? Impossible—otherwise, you wouldn't be reading this book. But if you were to judge American society solely by what you read in the press or see on TV, you'd have to assume that there are only two kinds of people in this country—heinous oppressors and hapless victims. It's the most simple-minded social analysis imaginable, but it's how we see ourselves portrayed every day. It's no wonder that some of our more softheaded citizens buy into that so completely. The rest of us just soak it up, mute with bewilderment—or loud with rage.*

# *Your Daily Newspaper Hates You*

—— ♦ ——

YOU PROBABLY THINK THAT A WORKING KNOWLEDGE OF THE ENGLISH language is all you need to be able to understand a newspaper, magazine, or news broadcast, right?

Wrong.

There's something else: you need to understand the presumptions that go into deciding what news *is* and how every story will be told.

What do I mean by "presumptions"? Please allow me the pleasure of explaining.

First, we must acknowledge that in order for something to be considered "news," it must satisfy certain requirements. Leaving out reports of fires, car crashes, train wrecks, murders, and war, and putting aside the spoon-fed pronouncements of government officials, "news" as defined by journalists today is the story of *conflict*. Usually, it's about conflict over rights, because that struggle is at the heart of any free society.

But when hearing of such a conflict, do the reporters and editors start their search for the truth in a totally unbiased, objective way? Do they actually investigate to see if an allegation holds up before they report it?

They'll *tell* you they do.

They'll vow, promise, swear, aver, and take an oath with one hand on the Bible that they do.

But they don't.

They listen to one side. They listen to the other. And from that they create a tale. It's always the same tale: an aggrieved party has been made to suffer at the hands of some supposedly more powerful entity who has been engaging in unfair, unjust behavior.

The complainer is always given a sympathetic hearing. He's always believed to be in the right unless proven otherwise, except that reporters don't spend much energy trying to disprove their own sources. If by some freakish chance the accuser *is* proven wrong, the story never runs.

The allegedly more powerful party always gets a skeptical hearing. He is always believed to be in the wrong, and if he attempts to refute the story it *still* runs. The fact that he denies something *proves* he has something to hide, right? And anyway, an accusation is "news" in itself today.

Why do journalists operate this way? I don't know. Maybe they're lazy. Maybe they're gullible. Maybe they think that working hard to track down the facts is beneath them. Maybe they have no idea of the damage a false accusation can do to the life of an innocent person. Maybe their own personal resentments lead them to automatically, unthinkingly side with those who call themselves underdogs, truth be damned.

Whatever. In order to understand the news, you must first know what today's journalists *presume* to be true even before they've checked out one fact. Feel free to take notes. This gets tricky.

> If a white man is in conflict with a black man—the white man is in the wrong.
> If a white man is in conflict with a white woman—the white man is in the wrong.
> If a black man is in conflict with a black woman—the black man is in the wrong.
> If a black man is in conflict with a white woman—the black man is in the wrong.
> If a white is in conflict with an Asian—the white is in the wrong.
> If an Asian is in conflict with a black—the Asian is in the wrong.

If a police officer is in conflict with a citizen—the cop is in the wrong.

If a Southerner is in conflict with a Northerner—the Southerner is in the wrong.

If a Midwesterner is in conflict with an Easterner—the Midwesterner is in the wrong.

If a heterosexual is in conflict with a homosexual—the heterosexual is in the wrong.

If an HIV-negative person is in conflict with an HIV-positive person—the HIV-negative person is in the wrong.

If a fully able person is in conflict with a handicapped person—the able person is in the wrong.

If an old person is in conflict with a young person—the old person is in the wrong.

If two people of different economic circumstances are in conflict—the richer person is in the wrong.

If a religious person is in conflict with an atheist—the religious person is in the wrong.

If a business is in conflict with an individual—the business is in the wrong.

If human rights are in conflict with animal rights—the human is in the wrong.

If a white is accused of racial discrimination—he or she is in the wrong.

If a black is accused of racial discrimination—the white is in the wrong.

If a man is accused of sexual harassment—the man is in the wrong.

If a woman is accused of sexual harassment—the man is in the wrong.

If government is in conflict with an individual—government is in the wrong.

If America is in conflict with another country—America is in the wrong.

If a Republican is in conflict with a Democrat—the Republican is in the wrong.

And finally, if a conservative is in conflict with a liberal—the conservative is always, I mean *always,* in the wrong.

Got it? Now you're ready to fully comprehend the so-called news-gathering organizations. They don't "gather" news. News stories aren't like acorns lying on the ground waiting for squirrels to "gather" them. The media *invent* news. They *decide* news. They *decree* news.

Can you tell that big-time elitist journalism is not my favorite American institution these days? I'm just sick of all the posturing, the deceit, the hypocrisy, the smug, self-absorbed arrogance these fools pump out every day. If you consume news the way most people do—meaning, if you believe what you read and see and hear without using any of your own powers of critical thinking and reason—then your idea of what's going on in the world is distorted and unbalanced and wrong. You're clueless. Of course, I could say that if you're too weak-headed to actually examine what you're being fed, then you deserve to eat garbage.

Look at *The New York Times*, for instance, the newspaper that almost all others slavishly emulate.

The *Times* is pathetic. Here's a newspaper that has the greatest coverage of the world, bar none, of any paper or magazine. No matter how remote the area, you can bet your bottom dollar that if there's a story, the *Times* will have excellent reportage.

And yet, the publisher and the editors of the mighty *New York Times* have a neurotic fixation that compels them to placate every politically correct cause they can find. They are blind to what is really going on in this country. Either that, or somebody in the Sulzberger family or the Ochs family left a legacy of guilt that the current owners are trying desperately to expiate.

The *Times* has an editorial policy that betrays this neurosis over and over again. The paper has an agenda that, if pursued to its logical extreme, would leave us a Third World nation, where any heterosexual white male would have to plead for forgiveness for his sins in order to survive.

In describing the 104th Congress, for instance, they'll routinely characterize it as mean-spirited or cruel. But cruel to *whom?* To those with their hands out for an allowance and some free cheese? Why is it the *Times* never sides with the vast majority of Americans, who are paying cruel, backbreaking taxes to fuel programs that actually destroy the middle class? The *Times*men have abandoned not only their readers and advertisers but even their own heritage. They strain to distance themselves from the great contributions of European society to polity, the arts, literature, science, exploration. As they exalt every malcontent "minority" with a complaint, they denigrate and flagellate themselves. They are ashamed to acknowledge that Europeans who happen to be white—and I don't know of any other kind—have made the most significant contribution to this country and the world.

*The New York Times itself,* on its best days, is a remarkable achievement of European-American culture. But instead of expressing confidence in that and encouraging others to follow their example, they delight in finding fault with their own legacy. It's a kind of institutional nihilism at work: The paper seeks to advance values that endanger its own survival.

The obsession with political correctness there permeates every inch of the paper now—even the sports page. Instead of labeling absurd the pressure to change the nickname of the St. John's basketball team and even though ninety percent of the alumni prefer the nickname Redmen, the *Times* says it's understandable that decent people want the name changed. Now they call the team the Red Storm.

The astounding thing is that the people who control our major media don't even consider their politics to be to the left of center. In their self-aggrandizement, in their pomposity, in their elitist snobbery, they think what they are advocating is simply the natural and desirable order of things. And, therefore, anybody who disagrees is an enemy of the people.

# Why Radio Talk
# Is So Wonderful
# and TV Talk Stinks

———— ◆ ————

TELEVISION WAS SUPPOSED TO HAVE BEEN AN ADVANCE ON RADIO, but it hasn't really worked out that way, has it?

Oh, technologically, I suppose, TV *does* go one step beyond radio. But how about content? TV was supposed to have opened up the world to us, to have taken us from our living rooms to every corner of the planet and beyond. It was to have turned us into the "global village."

Instead, TV fills our homes with mindlessness and drivel, twenty-four hours a day. This may be the global village, but all we ever see are the village idiots. The best way to witness how TV has failed on its promise to outdo radio is to compare how the two media handle discussion of the important matters of our lives. In other words, how they do *talk*.

Talk radio, for all its flaws, is about substantial issues. You can listen to any show and instantly be aware of the country's most urgent concerns, what the citizens fear and hope, what they love and hate. You may disagree with what's being said, but that only proves that something important is being discussed. In talk radio, the host is *required* to have strong opinions and be able to back them up with facts and reason.

And how about talk TV? Total trash. Freak shows. You know exactly what I mean. Do they reflect what's going on in our lives or our country? Not one bit, unless you think it's important to be reminded that we have a plentiful supply of halfwits and morally bankrupt cretins who behave like savages and then brag about it for the entertainment of millions of brain-dead strangers drooling before their TV sets.

Believe me, the Nobel Prize committee is never going to turn its attention to the hosts of talk radio shows. Still, we're a far sight better than slimeballs like Jenny Jones and Jerry Springer and all the rest.

At first, these shows were content to feature the most salacious, degrading talk imaginable. But that wasn't enough. They had to induce women and men to dress as scantily as the censors would allow. Then they got the inspiration to engineer the most humiliating, foul clashes between feuding pieces of human debris. Jenny Jones and her crew already set one murder in motion, and they're all still going strong.

The scummier these shows are, apparently, the bigger the ratings. But where will it end? After a while people are going to say, "Hey, I saw that sick perversion on Ricki Lake last week! Show me some new sleaze!" Next will we witness a murder right there, on the air? Instead of simply hearing about it, will we get to *watch* some mother seduce her teenage daughter's boyfriend? When they invite some depraved child molester on the show, will they stage a dramatic re-creation of his ghastly crime?

It sounds crazy today, sure; but once upon a time, so did everything else they've done. And they call talk radio dangerous.

I know how stupid and phony television is from firsthand experience. In 1969, I was doing *The Bob Grant Show* on KLAC Radio. But John Kluge wanted to sell the station's parent company, Metromedia, and in preparation for that, he decided to get out of the controversy business. No more talk radio, he decreed. The station went to country music or some such format. It was no longer a place I could call home.

At the same time, a local TV interview show called *Tempo* was looking for a cohost. I auditioned for the job and got it. The producers liked me because they could throw people from any walk of life my way and without missing a beat, I could interview them. I could segue smoothly from the treasurer of the state of California to Ernest Borgnine.

My cohost was an actress named Jeanie Baird. Her career never went far, but the chemistry between us was good, and the show was popular.

One day, our opening guest was the actress, Marlo Thomas. At this time, she wasn't a big star yet. Jeanie was doing the interview, and I was sitting quietly off to the side, listening. Thomas had said that she had a sign that always inspired and sustained her, a poster or something that read, "Remember, today is the first day of the rest of your life." Pretty inane as slogans go, but it worked for her, I guess.

Then, suddenly, Jeanie hit a dry spot. It sometimes happens to interviewers; for the life of you, you can't think of a single question to ask. In her desperation, she turned to me and said, "Bob, maybe you have a question for Marlo?"

"Well, yes, yes, as a matter of fact, I do," I said, trying to cover. "You know, Marlo, some people watching this might be surprised to hear that you need a slogan to sustain you in your work. They might say, 'Well, gee, Marlo Thomas doesn't need that. She's the daughter of a famous man.' Maybe there are people who feel you've had everything dumped into your lap."

And she said, "Who are *you* to say that? How *dare* you talk to me that way!"

So I said, "Well, who are *you?* You can't answer a reasonable question!"

I could feel Jeanie and everybody else go into shock. I had broken the unwritten rule of TV: never allow anything genuine on the air. Never treat a celebrity with anything other than total worship.

Well, somehow we got through the program. Next thing I hear is that Jane Fonda canceled out for the following day. Thomas had called her and reported the treatment she received. Then Danny Thomas called the show's director and yelled and hollered and threatened to break my legs. A few more stars began canceling, too. I quit a week or so later. It's funny now. I was good at TV, but inside I'm not built to be as phony as the medium demands.

Actually, the first sign of that came a little before the Marlo Thomas debacle. I was interviewing a guy who was a homosexual and a minister. And I said, on the air, "You know, I cannot even call you 'Reverend.' I just can't conceive of a man of the cloth being a homosexual.''

Between him and Marlo Thomas, they drove me out of that stupid industry, thank God. The guy who took my place on that show managed it a little better than I did—Regis Philbin is *still* doing pretty well on the boob tube. He's welcome to it.

# The Devil and
# Mr. Grant

———— ◆ ————

PICTURE THIS SALACIOUS SPECTACLE: OVER ONE HUNDRED NORMAL looking, middle-class American women filing into a Times Square porno theater to watch a dirty movie—the real thing, with wall-to-wall explicit sex. They're being led inside by the equally normal-looking middle-aged man who enticed them all into this seamy escapade.

Now, because I am such a fine and decent and upstanding fellow, you might be surprised that I even *know* of such a tawdry event. If so, you'll be truly shocked to learn that the man leading those innocent matrons into the theater, the instigator of this depraved entertainment, was yours truly.

It started, as so many of my adventures do, with a telephone call to my radio program. It was in the early seventies, and we were discussing *Last Tango in Paris,* the Marlon Brando movie. And I got a call from a lady who wondered what all the fuss was about concerning pornographic movies and why a respected actor like Marlon Brando had made one.

I told her that I had seen *Last Tango,* that it was a bore that flopped at the box office, and that it wasn't a typical X-rated movie, anyway. And she said, "Well, I don't understand—it was rated X." I said, "Yeah, but it didn't show explicit sex." "Well," she replied, "how explicit *are* they?" I said, "You've never heard of *Deep Throat* or *Behind the Green Door?*" By then both those films had become emblems for the whole industry.

And she said, "Well, I've never seen them, but I'd like to."

I said, "Listen, I'll tell you what. Ask your husband to take you."

"I'm a widow," she replied.

"Well," I said, "go alone or go with a friend and see for yourself."

"Oh, I couldn't do *that,*" she answered. "I'd be too embarrassed."

So finally I said, "I'll tell you what—I'm going away on vacation tomorrow. If you don't get anybody to take you in the meantime, let me know when I get back and *I'll* take you."

And I never gave it another thought—until I came back from vacation and found my desk piled high with cards and letters from women who wanted to go with me to a porno movie. Hey, I thought, this could be fun. So I called a guy at a notorious theater on 49th Street, and I said, "How would you like it if some matinee I came in with a hundred or so women?"

"Great!" he said. "You can all be my guests."

So I announced this field trip on the air, a free porno movie for any woman. I only invited women, because if men were there, my guests might feel inhibited. And one hundred and twenty-eight of them showed up at the studio on the appointed afternoon. We strolled down Seventh Avenue together, right into the theater. There were about four or five guys in raincoats already seated, waiting for the show to begin, and they almost went into shock. All of a sudden, scores of women—old, young, on crutches—began taking their seats.

The lights dimmed. The movie started. To this day I remember the title—*The Afternoons of Pamela Mann*. Right from the first scene I began to sink in my seat. As the seconds crawled by, I sunk lower and lower. Because the very first thing you saw was a scene on a pool table. There was this girl engaging in fellatio on a guy while another guy was having intercourse with her. A third man was ejaculating all over her. I mean, it was the most debauched scene you could want.

I could feel the entire theater tense up. Nobody breathed. I think half of them were in shock. Two women started arguing. I heard one say, "Well, what did you expect?! You knew that's what this was going to be!" But they all stayed, except for one woman, a Jamaican lady who said, "Oh, I— I—I'm gonna stand in the lobby." And she did. But all the other women stayed and watched the movie. They learned a few things that day, I'll venture. And then we went back to the studio and had a rousing roundtable discussion of what we saw.

I remember asking the woman who came on crutches why she had wanted to see the show. And she said, "Look at me. Who would want me? What fun can I have? It was a little excitement for me." Most of the women thanked me. They said they had often wondered what the heck it was like. Some of them, obviously, had seen them before—some of them had boyfriends, some of them were married—but most of them were women who were alone. And they thanked me, like I did them a favor.

I organized two more porno theater trips later on. Every once in a while a woman would call or write and say, "When are you gonna take us to the movies again?" I have to confess that I didn't think it was any big deal. I mean, here it was, the 1970s—the sexual revolution. Naturally, I got mail from some people who said, "And you call yourself a conservative!" I told them I never called myself a conservative. I don't mind if others call me a conservative. But I'm just me.

In fact, this wasn't my only contact with the world of pornographic movies. Back when it was still a novelty, I had interviewed a director, Lou Campo, who had made such a film, something titled *Lickety Split.* I had gone to see it to prepare for my interview, and later he asked if I would give it a promotional blurb. And I said, "Well, okay"—and I gave a statement to the effect that if you want to see an X-rated movie, see this one, because it has elements of humor and plot, in addition to what you'd expect to see.

Not too long after, this guy was busted because his film was being shown in Queens. I mean, New York is a strange

place, in a way, because if you're in Manhatten anything
goes, but if you're in Queens, look out. He was facing a five-
year jail term, so his attorney came to me and said that they
were trying to establish that the movie hadn't violated community standards. And the attorney was hoping that the
court would accept me as a fair judge of what community
standards were.

I actually testified on behalf of the director. But, lo and
behold, the prosecutor said, "You say you're a disinterested
observer of the scene?" I said, "Well, I'm disinterested to the
extend that I've no involvement with this motion picture."

He said, "Ah, but you *do.*" And with that he produced
copies of the *New York Post* and the New York *Daily News,*
both of which had ads containing my blurb. So it backfired
on the guy, and he was convicted.

I have mixed feelings about pornography. On the one hand,
I don't want the police going into somebody's living room
and confiscating a videotape or a magazine. And yet, I think
we've become too obsessed with sexual license, to the general detriment of our public life. If that sounds to you like a
contradiction, you're right—life is full of contradictions.

Look, we've had pornography from time immemorial. And
we're not going to wipe it out, nor do I want to see it wiped
out. I don't want to see it flaunted; I don't want to see children with it, because they're not capable of handling it. Banning it now would be like Prohibition all over again. If we
can handle alcohol in an adult way, we can live with pornography, too. I'm more of a realist on a lot of these issues than
most conservatives are. And as long as it's not flaunted, as
long as it's not involving children, then a person who wants
a videotape or magazine should have it. It's his or her business, not yours, and *definitely* not mine.

My attitude toward prostitution is similarly schizophrenic.
On the one hand, it disgusts me. On the other, we know that
it is the oldest profession. We know that there will always
be women who will sell their sex, and men who will buy it.
So I wonder, why don't we accept it, once and for all, and
stop this silly game of putting our resources into the so-called
vice squad? We're such hypocrites. We don't want to get our

hands dirty. We don't mind getting *other* parts of our bodies dirty, but not our hands.

And what would dirty our hands? Acknowledging that prostitution exists for a reason and then decriminalizing it. Notice I don't suggest we *legalize* it, because that would be tantamount to approval. And we don't have to approve, only accept. How much better off we'd be if prostitutes had to register with the police or some city agency and have periodic health checkups, and operated in certain areas only. So that people who complain about being importuned by streetwalkers could begin to live in peace.

I've interviewed many hookers during my career on the radio. The last prostitute I interviewed—on the telephone—works for the Chicken Ranch in Nevada. There's a perfect example of a community that was realistic enough to say, "Hey, look, we've got prostitutes; they're roaming all around Las Vegas and Reno. Let's admit it and deal with it like adults." And so parts of Nevada allow these brothels.

You know, there are some people who feel that *all* women are prostitutes. Some women are honest enough to say, "I'm a prostitute, and it will cost you X number of dollars to go to bed with me." Others will only say, "Oh, you want me to be your girlfriend? Okay, buy me this, give me that, take me there."

I knew a fellow once, a politician, who was always talking about his beautiful young girlfriend. He used to say, over and over, "I don't know what she sees in me."

Well, what *did* she in him? Only this: He put her in a nice apartment. He bought her good clothes. He took her to the best restaurants and to shows and on vacations. *That's* what she saw in him. And as soon as he hit hard times—which he did—and could no longer be as generous with her as he once was, she dropped him like a used condom. But until that sad day, he used to go on as though he really believed she saw something handsome, irresistible, charming about him. Dream on! Was she a prostitute? In my book, yes, she was, though I'm sure she (and my acquaintance) would disagree strongly.

I think some men go to prostitutes because they want sexual gratification without having to go through the torture of seducing the woman. I'm told that sex today is very available, very free, without any of the strings that were attached back when I was a young stud. Still, I guess, some men don't want to have to do what's necessary to get sex on a woman's terms.

Other men go to hookers because they're not getting the emotional thrill they used to get from sex with their wives. When I was young, I knew a man in Chicago who told me that he no longer could get aroused by his wife—who was fairly attractive—because she was the mother of his children. Somehow or other, since she had become a mother, he was unable to feel lust for her. And, you know, we like to play games with ourselves: We like to talk about how great love is, and how if you love someone then the sex must be wonderful. That's very idealistic and romantic, and I don't belittle it as a concept. I think it's a wonderful fantasy. But why must people then deny their capacity for another emotion—less noble, perhaps, but nevertheless very strong? It also begins with the letter *L*: L-U-S-T. Why are we afraid—men *and* women—to admit that love and lust are two different things, and that both exist within each and every one of us?

We had a poor excuse for a president of the United States who said, "Ah have lusted in my heart." Remember when Jimmy Peanut said that in *Playboy?* That was like when another president told us, "Ah didn't inhale." They want you to believe that while they feel the attraction of sinful behavior, they're strong enough to resist it. That they're above actually *doing* it. What a load of crap.

# *The Rise and Rise of the Great Inevitable One*

◆

EVEN SIMPLY ATTEMPTING TO WRITE THIS CHAPTER MAY PROVE TO be the dumbest decision I could make in my brand-new career as an author. I mean it—I could come out of this looking pretty bad, like a jealous, petty whiner with a mouthful of sour grapes.

Oh, what the hell. I'll give it a whack.

A few years ago, I was visiting my son out in California, and he had a business call to make while I was with him. He introduced me to his client, saying, "This is my dad, Bob Grant. He does talk radio in New York."

And she said, "Oh . . . yes? Huh, I see." Clearly, a woman who didn't know me from Adam.

Then I spotted it in her hand. A book that created at least a medium-sized revolution in publishing, the knock-down, drag-out, certifiably phenomenal, mega-hit monster best-seller that was everywhere you looked at the time, from sea to shining sea and all points in between. A book that just happened to have been written by a fellow right-of-center talk-radio figure, a man who needs no introduction, whose kindly round face, staring out from the book jacket, is by now as recognizable as any movie star's.

You may have heard of him.

I said to the woman, "Well, you'd know who I was if you'd read that book."

"Oh, I've read it," she said.

"Then you didn't read page thirteen very closely," I said.

We turned to the page, whereupon she read the author's description of yours truly. He wrote that I am "the king of talk radio in New York. . . . He is one of the few talk show hosts who has lasted in combat radio. He defined it and spawned countless imitators all over the country. Nobody does it better than he does and his ratings are proof. If New York is an argument, and it is, then Bob Grant's show is New York every day."

And—*dammit!*—the woman instantly began to look upon me with a whole new respect and admiration. Even worse: I had revealed my shameful secret, that I'd actually *memorized* the number of the page on which the author lavished me with praise.

Is there any higher compliment I can pay him?

Oh, wait, maybe this: When I surf through TV channels with my remote control, I must be ever vigilant just in case I accidently come upon a station that's carrying his show. Because the mere sight of him, and the knowledge that countless millions of Americans are absolutely riveted to the screen when his presence graces it, can send me into a funk. I also have to be on guard walking through malls and airports, lest I spy a store window displaying his books or magazines whose covers feature his image. I've given up trying to get through a newspaper without tripping over his name a dozen or so times.

There—is it possible to heap my praise any higher?

To explain all this angst, let's flash back for a moment to a time twenty or so years ago. I was doing pretty much the same show I do now—abrasive and hateful to some, gratifying and highly entertaining to others, but unmistakably, inarguably, guaranteed-one-hundred-percent *conservative.* Back when we were still scuffling over issues like forced busing and the Soviet plan for world domination, I was the *only* broadcaster in town (or anywhere else, for that matter) who espoused the rock-ribbed conservative point of view and got good ratings doing it.

It might seem like it was a lonely life, but to be honest, I loved being out there on my own. Every other media figure was mouthing the idiotic liberal line (this was New York in its lefty Democratic heyday, remember). And I was different. Special. Maybe even unique. I had a true-blue following of listeners who used to say, "Bob, if we didn't have you, we wouldn't have *anything*." This stuff made it all worthwhile.

And things remained that way until some time during Ronald Reagan's terms in the White House. That's when conservatism began to take on a certain glamour, an undeniable vigor. We were no longer being misrepresented as a bunch of gun nuts, Birchers, antifluoridation freaks, apocalypse junkies, closet Klansmen, and crazed paranoiacs. It's clear, looking back, that the conservative point of view lacked but one thing—a leading man.

It was only a matter of time, of course. That's why, even now, I need refer to him only as The Great Inevitable One for you to know whom I mean.

I still remember my first eyeful of the flier announcing his arrival here from a station in Sacramento. Well, well, I thought, some young conservative buck is trying to start up a network talk-radio show. The satellite technology, finally, was in place to allow such a thing. Good luck to him.

Then he himself arrived in town. Among his first stops was a visit to me. He was a true gentleman. I remember his words: "Your reputation precedes you, sir," he said.

Did what followed all happen overnight? It seems that way to me now. But how?

Well, first of all, the satellite made him the first *national* media figure who dared to refuse to spout the liberal party line. Every American who had grown sick of the knee-jerk lefties who run broadcasting raised a cheer when they heard him speak. And people like tuning in to someone who's being heard all across the country. It gives listeners the sense that they're part of something truly *big*.

Second, and most important, he did his show with a sense of humor. It signaled how low the liberal philosophy had fallen when, instead of railing and raging against it, people began to *laugh* at it. For years, liberals had mocked conservatives. Now, finally, the shoe was on the other foot, and it fit just fine. He confounded the stereotype of how a conservative sounded: he was downright amiable and amused. His delivery, his voice—all easy on the ears. He likes to call himself "just a lovable fuzzball," and he really is, professionally and personally.

But did he *have* to attract twenty million fanatic followers? Did he *have* to inspire such devotion, such loyalty, that his fans would snap up books, coffee mugs, T-shirts, and anything else with his handsome visage on it? Did he *have* to become practically synonymous with the revitalized brand of conservatism that's getting this country back on the right track? Did he *have* to turn into a national obsession?

Even worse, because broadcasting is essentially a followers' medium, his success has inspired the proliferation of more public conservatives on TV, radio, and in print than I can count. Now people say to me, "We wouldn't have anybody on our side, Bob, if it weren't for you . . . and that guy and that guy and that guy and that guy . . ."

Of course, I am a big enough person to acknowledge that while he may have made my life a little less special, he has done more for the conservative cause than anybody realizes. In fact, I truly believe that if he wants to put all his influence to good use, he would take a leading role in the elections this year. Maybe even run for something. Maybe even president. I have no doubt he'd win. But that job would leave him no time at all for a radio show.

Rush in ninety-six!

211

# The Most Disgusting Sound on Radio Today

◆

THERE'S LIVING PROOF THAT THE MOST IMPORTANT FACTOR IN THE life of a successful person is the timing of his birth, and its name is Howard Stern.

If he had come into radio twenty years earlier, his brand of "humor" would have earned him a fast ticket home. Twenty years from now, the airwaves will be so degraded that nothing will shock us. This is not a reflection on him—he didn't decide when to be born—but on what he has to offer to American listeners today.

If you've never had the pleasure of hearing his show, I can describe its singular defining characteristic: He's famous for turning unpleasant natural functions into his own signature sounds. He fetishizes what the rest of us would never even mention *off* the air. He's like a baby digging around delightedly in his own diaper.

That he has become rich and famous for doing that tells me how low we have sunk. He's probably the most popular figure in radio today, so what does that say about us? Nothing good, I assure you.

He prides himself on his fearlessness, but he displayed his true nature when the Latino singer Selena was murdered. He actually found something to laugh about in that tragedy. Then, when her fans protested, he whined that he was only making fun of Latino music, not of her death. Which is a lie, pure and simple: During his "commentary" on what happened, he played Mexican music overdubbed with the sound of gunshots. He's a hypocrite and a coward.

So, I find him disgusting, but I have to admit there have been times he's made me laugh. He's actually capable of intelligent, biting mockery of political correctness and hypersensitivity about race and ethnicity. But that's not why he's famous. His success is due mainly to his favorite four-letter word, which starts with an F and ends with a T and reminds me of nothing so much as the sound of Howard Stern's voice.

# *Academia Nuts*

———— ◆ ————

THERE'S BUT ONE PLACE LEFT ON THE FACE OF THE EARTH WHERE widespread belief in the goodness and rightness of the principles of communism still endures. It's not in Russia or anywhere else in what was the Soviet Union. It's not in Cuba, that's for certain, or in Angola or Mozambique or Prague or Warsaw or Vietnam, either. You'll guess incorrectly all day if I let you, so I'll end the mystery now:

It's in American universities.

It's been said, only half-facetiously, that there are more communists on the campuses of America than there ever were in Red Square.

Now, I'm not talking about card-carrying members of the Communist Party USA or KGB spies or anything like what went on in academia when it still looked like the reds had a shot at ruling the world. I'm talking about philosophical communists. All-talk communists. Lip-service commies of the heart, mind, and soul.

The cruelly enforced egalitarianism and anti-elitism of Stalin and Mao are still going strong on campus. So are the virulent anti-Americanism and anticapitalism. And the refusal to allow dissent or free and open exchanges of opinion hearkens back to the days when the threat of the gulag kept millions under mental lock and key. The thought-thugs who staff America's colleges like to think of themselves as the party rulers, and the students as the proletariat.

It's almost hilarious—until you remember that those students are our future, and we're paying the tab for these academic exercises in tyranny and nihilism.

I remember when I took my freshman social studies course, the inevitable 101. The teacher was a woman, Miss Franklin, and even though I was an innocent babe, I looked at her on the first day of class and said to myself, "This ugly broad is a pinko red commie." And in fact, whenever she would say "Soviet Union" or "Joseph Stalin" or "the New Deal," she would smile.

Then, lo and behold, years later I was reading a book that named members of the Communist Party USA, and whose name did I find? I thought, how many other Miss Franklins must there be out there teaching young people? Maybe they weren't all staunch party members, but what were they teaching? Which value system were they praising? What were they doing to rewrite history?

These were the same American intellectuals who couldn't bring themselves to condemn Stalin even after communist totalitarianism had been unmasked in the eyes of the rest of the world. Faithful reds in eastern Europe, Italy, France, Spain, and elsewhere turned their backs on the cause after the 1968 Czechoslovakian Spring, when Russian troops crushed freedom in that gentle country. In the U.S., though, nothing changed. Lillian Hellman never denounced Stalin, and she was but one of many highbrows who refused to see communism for what it truly was.

I have come to the conclusion that the American communists believed in their cause not because they hoped it would improve their country, but because they hoped it would destroy it. They weren't really *for* socialism. They were just *against* democracy and capitalism and freedom. Our communists, unlike those elsewhere, just hated *any* system that worked. Like most Americans, our commies were apolitical. They were espresso anarchists—misfits, malcontents, and neurotics.

The current crop of professors—the deconstructionists, the postconstructionists, the New History and New Criticism crowd—are the intellectual heirs to those losers. Academia is now a dangerous place for a youngster to go, because he or she can pick up some nasty misinformation. College kids call me on the air all the time now. Now so long ago, a young person wouldn't be caught dead calling a show like mine. That they do is evidence of the kind of mistreatment they're getting at school.

They'll call and tell me how they're being taught, for instance, that the United States was responsible for the Cold War. How, as communism fell, the United States was trying to undermine stability in the Soviet Union. Just the opposite of what really went on.

Or they'll report that they're made to feel that they live in occupied territory or that Christopher Columbus was one of history's worst war criminals. Young white males in particular say they're treated as though they've done something horribly wrong, that they're responsible for current as well as historical oppression of blacks and Latinos and women and homosexuals.

Today, courses in history, political science, literature, sociology, and other disciplines are being taught by "ethnic studies" instructors. Can anybody explain the logic in that? Or in something called "gay and lesbian studies"? Since when is history either gay *or* straight? Since when is literature black, brown, yellow, *or* white? If "sociology" is not a woman, why is it being taught under the heading of "women's studies"? At this rate, we'll never again have a course simply titled American History. We'll have courses in white female history, white male history (maybe), black female history, black male history, gay white female history, gay black female history, disabled gay white female history, fragrance-sensitive disabled gay black female history, and so on. Any day now, I swear, high school kids will be required to study bisexual algebra.

These are not studies. This is not scholarship. It's a flimsy grab bag of courses that should be titled "Feel-Good-About-Yourself 101," "Advanced Let's-Pander-to-Minorities-So-They-Won't-Occupy-the-Dean's-Office," and "Introduction to Give-Unqualified-Students-the-False-Sense-That-They're-Getting-an-Education." It's no coincidence that the rise of ethnic and gender studies was accompanied by the advent of speech codes on campus, those loathsome rules that prohibit freedom of expression in order to keep somebody's tender feelings from getting bruised.

When I went to school, we were encouraged to believe that our ethnicity, race, gender, or religion were all immaterial. We were taught that who we were inside was all that would count as we made our way through life. Today, students are being taught just the opposite—that who they are as individuals is meaningless and that only differences in race and background determine who we *really* are. How will that help resolve the divisiveness currently afflicting our country? It won't. In fact, it will make things far worse in the future.

Another difference from when I went to school is that back then, we had to *learn*. We had to take real courses, in science and mathematics and the humanities, where we were expected to absorb information and ideas. Sounds quaint, doesn't it? All the current academic concentration on grievances has effectively moved the focus off of *learning*. College today isn't about learning, you see. It's there to help our campus commies to advance beliefs that the rest of the thinking world has been laughing at for more than four decades.

# *American Psychobabble*

— ◆ —

A FAIR NUMBER OF AMERICANS ARE RICH ENOUGH TO BE BEYOND having to worry about survival and solvency. A smaller set within that group are also widely adored, worshipped, admired figures who receive more than their fair share of attention. That crowd—actors, artists, certain tycoons, some politicians and media types, the A-list—would seem to have it all. They have managed to fulfill the two most basic human hungers, for sustenance and love.

There's something else they have in common: they all seem to need psychiatrists.

Honestly, when was the last time you read about one of these fortunate figures without reading about their dependence upon some analyst or therapist of one sort or another? Some see their shrink five days a week. Some continue going for years and years. "My shrink, my shrink, my shrink . . ." they blather on.

Here's my question—what exactly do these individuals need to have *shrunk?*

A cynic might say their salaries and egos are what require a little downsizing. If they had to live like mere mortals and worry about things like tuition bills and promotions at the office and mortgage and car and insurance payments, maybe they'd have less time and energy for such self-absorption.

If I may play the psychiatrist for a moment, I'll put forth my guess. I believe what they need to shrink is the emptiness inside them. If you're destined to live the mundane life of a working stiff or a middle-class desk jockey, you can still harbor the fantasy that riches and fame would turn your existence into a bowl of cherries. Once you actually *get* the fortune and the adulation, though, that fantasy pops like a soap bubble. You learn that you're still the same old person, with most of the same old problems and woes. The emptiness is the space formerly occupied by dreams.

I recall reading a biography of a truly fine actor who was a truly pathetic, pitiable human being, one who suffered from the moment he was born until his premature death. I'm talking about Montgomery Clift. Throughout the book, the author talked about the consuming emptiness that Clift felt.

I can contrast all of the great, miserable celebrities I've met and known with other, ordinary people who seem to be genuinely satisfied and happy. Believe it or not, shock of shocks, the happy people seem to be those who are living for someone or something other than themselves.

It's the self-centered, narcissistic, spoiled, overindulged celebrities who can afford the luxury of thinking only of themselves and their careers. How *could* they be happy? They see psychiatrists hoping to find a rationale for their unhappiness. "My mother didn't breast-feed me . . . My father was distant . . . Our family was dysfunctional . . . I'm bipolar . . ." You've heard all the excuses by now.

I think that the original version of psychoanalysis as pioneered by Freud was a valid attempt to help people learn about themselves. It wasn't intended to get people off the hook for their problems, but that's what it has turned into. We used to depend on friends and family to give us a sympathetic hearing when things went wrong. Now people hire professionals to serve the same purpose. Look, Americans hire people to care for their aging parents, nurture their children, help them exercise, and everything else. Why should this be different?

The dangerous aspect of this misuse of psychiatry is in criminal matters. If you commit a run-of-the-mill crime, you're stuck with it, but if you do something truly horrendous, you hire a shrink to say it's not your fault. You pay him to testify, "This individual committed the crime not because he is an enemy of society, not because he is a danger to innocent people, but because he is a troubled person. His psyche is wounded, and it's our responsibility to heal that wound, so that he can take his rightful place in society."

In the Dark Ages, we used to blame evil deeds on demonic possession. In the age of individualism, we placed the responsibility squarely on the criminal himself. Now we've come full circle. Instead of priests, we've got shrinks. Instead of Satan, we've got society. In both extremes, we deny the freedom of choice each of us truly possesses. That's what psychiatry's role today is—to tell people somebody else is to blame for their unhappiness.

# Fired Again

———— ◆ ————

RADIO ANNOUNCERS MAY BE GOOD OR BAD, SMART OR DUMB, LIB-eral or conservative, decent or slimy, but there's one thing almost all of us have in common.

We all get fired.

It happens for a variety of reasons—format changes, bum ratings, new ownership, bad blood, controversies, on-air feuds, salary disputes, contract squabbles, nervous break-downs—you name it and it's happened. Hollywood execu-tives don't move around as often as radio people. I know announcers who have more miles on them than a migrant farmworker's Vega.

Perversely, some radio people wear their firings like a badge of honor, but I don't. It makes me uncomfortable to know that I'm doing anything on somebody else's terms. And just the word—"fired"—sounds like a violent and unhappy experience.

So while I don't brag about it, I have been fired from more than one radio job. Thankfully, I *can* say that it's never been because I wasn't pulling strong ratings. In fact, it's happened because when I say what I think, *everybody* hears it.

The greatest injustice of this sort befell me when I was in the employ of WOR, here in New York. What made it even worse was that I was prohibited from telling anyone my side of the story—until now, that is.

I agreed to work at WOR only because my previous employer, the idiotic R. Peter Straus, of WMCA, reneged on my contract, which means one thing and one thing only: He failed to hand over the pay increases he had agreed to.

I told him that if he didn't live up to his agreement, I'd feel free to entertain other offers. I guess he didn't take me seriously. At the time, WOR's star, Barry Farber, had announced he was leaving radio in order to run for mayor of New York. And the program director there called to ask if I was free to discuss a job. I didn't like Farber's time slot, 11:30 P.M., but it was a huge station, and the money potential was there, so when they offered the job, I took it.

I immediately told my bosses at WMCA. I offered to stay on for two weeks so they could line up a replacement. Just make today's show your last one, they ordered.

Fine and dandy by me. When I went on the air that day, doing my afternoon drive-time show, our newscaster said his usual line—"Now, let's get back to Bob Grant." But on this day I replied, "Bert, that's the last time you'll be saying that, because I am announcing that I am going to leave WMCA."

Well, there was pandemonium!

Suddenly, people began appearing in the control room. Management sent in a guy to sit in the studio, just in case I walked out or went off the wall and began spewing wildly. To be honest, it gave me a certain amount of satisfaction to say what I said on the air. But I was professional about it. I went on to thank all my colleagues at the station, and I even thanked that buffoon Peter Straus for giving me a shot at coming to New York. *Never* did I say that I'd be going to another station in town or mention anything at all about my new employer. That would have been a bush-league move. And it wasn't as though I had wanted to switch stations. I felt forced out by their holding back on the raise they promised.

My contract at WOR soon proved to be quite lucrative. It provided for healthy raises if I got high ratings, and sure enough, I got them, higher than management had anticipated. So the new show was a hit and I was happy.

But the station was owned by a company that was loaded with problems having nothing to do with me. Which meant that the minute I got the station into hot water, which I am incapable of avoiding, they'd fold like a cheap camera.

It didn't take long.

At about this time, the New York gubernatorial race was heating up. I didn't exactly campaign against Hugh Carey, but I made no secret of my distaste for him. One big issue of the campaign had to do with the candidates' financial disclosures. One day I got a call from a lawyer who said, "Bob, you have a reputation as a champion of citizens' rights. I'd like you to sign a petition I want to file, an order to show cause, in superior court, that would force Perry Duryea, the Republican candidate, to make public his 1976 taxes, and Hugh Carey, the Democrat, to reveal the campaign expenditures from his 1974 campaign."

Now, I wanted to sign that thing—Carey and Duryea were each attacking the other for hiding their financial information, so I figured we'd force them both to come clean. But before I signed it, I went to one of the executives at the station to get his approval. I explained the petition, and he asked, "Well, *how* will you sign it? As a private citizen or as a representative of this station?"

"I'm signing it as Robert Grant, private citizen," I assured him, and he said there'd be no problem. So I signed the petition, but the second I did, I got a queasy feeling in my stomach.

The next day, every television and radio news show and every newspaper in town carried the story—"Bob Grant, WOR radio commentator, has entered a petition, an order to show cause, *blah blah blah.*" Now, when Hugh Carey heard about that, he called the president of the parent company, and he said, "What is this so-and-so trying to do to me?" His opponent, Perry Duryea, *also* called the president and said, "What is this so-and-so trying to do to me?" At which point the man probably figured: "We have enough problems without this guy. He got the governor *and* his challenger mad at us. We don't need this."

So the president called WOR's station manager, Rick Devlin, who was in Chicago on business, and he said words to this effect: "Devlin, fire this skunk." Devlin pointed out that I was bringing in a lot of money. A lot of trouble, too, the president said. Fire him. Devlin promised to do it the second he returned to New York, but even that wasn't good enough—fly back right now and fire him, the man ordered.

When Devlin got into town, I was blissfully unaware, speaking to the Kiwanis Club of Flushing. While I was delivering my talk, the restaurant manager came up and put a little note on the lectern. It said: *"Call your office."* I concluded my speech, grabbed a phone, and spoke to my producer.

"Bob, Devlin wants to meet you at four o'clock," he said.

"What's up?" I asked.

"Gee, I don't know. Maybe you're going to get the afternoon-drive gig."

"Hey, great," I replied.

At four o'clock I walked into Rick Devlin's office. I never even had a chance to sit down. "Well, listen," he said, "I'm not going to beat around the bush. Effective immediately, we're canceling your show."

Knowing that the ratings were sky-high and that the revenue was great, I said, "But why?"

"I don't have to tell you why," he replied. "We're just canceling it."

I was shocked. "When do I do my last one?" I finally managed to say.

"You did it last night," he said.

I just couldn't believe that this was happening. It was bad enough that I had been fired, but not to get even one reason? And no matter who asked, the station refused to say why I was given the axe.

So there I was—out on the bricks.

The general manager of WNEW wanted to hire me. But his boss said, "No—that guy's trouble." The program director at my old station, WMCA, figured they'd get their ratings back if they rehired me. But Peter Straus's wife Ellen, who was running the station, said, "Oh, no—you haven't suffered enough yet. We won't take you back."

I was so furious that I was about to go on Barry Gray's radio show to tell what had happened to me. But then I was told that if I spoke about it, WOR would stop paying me what they owed on my contract. Only because I like eating better than talking did I swallow my pride and button my lip.

They actually ran me out of town. After a few months and no offers, I reluctantly agreed to take a job on a talk station in Philadelphia. The station, WWDB, was very nice to me. I asked the boss there, Dolly Banks, whether she was afraid of what would happen if I did my usual show there. Because I wasn't going to be doing anything any different.

"We want vintage Bob Grant," she assured me. I gave it to them, too, and they gave me a great year. I almost didn't come back to New York, I was so happy there in the birthplace of liberty.

But I had to return, if only to show people that I wasn't made of poison. I wanted everybody to know the real reason I was fired, what skunks they were at WOR. And yet I couldn't say a word. It must have really bothered Rick Devlin to do what he did, because a couple of years later, at Ronald Reagan's first inaugural ball, I ran into Devlin, and he wanted to talk to me. I wouldn't even look at him, but he chased me all over the room, insisting that we shake hands. Finally I said that I'd shake, but only if he'd tell me what had really happened. He promised he would—not then and there, he said, but next time we spoke. I never pursued it. You know why? *I no longer care!*

# And Again

———— ◆ ————

The headlines read: "GRANT TOPPLES WABC AS WOR SOARS TO THE TOP;" "WOR SCORES BIG;" "WOR SCORES BIG VICTORY, THANKS TO GRANT." Here I am back on the air at WOR, 710 on your radio dial. And how did I get here? Why am I here? Am I enjoying the fact that I have put WOR back on the map as a major player in the New York market once again? Frankly, yes. There is a great satisfaction in having achieved such tremendous success. But the way I got here was something I would not recommend to anyone.

"What happened?" people ask me all the time. Well, all right. You are going to hear it for the first time, directly from me.

It was April 3, 1996, at about 4:20 in the afternoon. I was on the air at WABC, talking to a familiar telephone caller by the name of Carl. Carl of Oyster Bay. I do not know Carl of Oyster Bay personally, but he is someone whom I will never forget.

Carl called in to talk about the recent plane crash in Bosnia, and the fact that Ron Brown, who was aboard that ill-fated plane, was under investigation at the time of the crash. Brown, the late former secretary of commerce, was under scrutiny for three separate matters, any or all of which could have led to an indictment, and possibly a conviction with a prison term. Let's face it—Ron Brown was a very suspicious character. Even a number of his heartiest supporters winced at some of the allegations that were being made against him.

At any rate, Carl of Oyster Bay was commenting on the fact that Ron Brown's death might spare Bill Clinton from embarrassment in the upcoming election. After all, Brown was one of Clinton's staunchest, most ardent supporters, had been the chairman of the Democratic National Committee, and was chosen by Clinton to be his commerce secretary. How could Bill Clinton turn away from one of his most loyal men? Well, Bill Clinton didn't have to worry about turning away from his man, because his man was quite dead.

Of course, at the time, we didn't know for sure that Brown was dead. During the course of the conversation with Carl of Oyster Bay, my producer came in to turn on CNN on the television set we had in the studio, to see if there were any new developments from the crash scene. I looked up at the screen to see a newscaster reporting that one survivor may have been pulled from the wreckage.

Noticing this, I said, "Hey Carl, I see that one survivor may have been pulled from the wreckage. You know, I have a hunch—now, this is just a gut feeling, but I have a hunch— that that one survivor is Ron Brown." I paused, and said, "Of course, at heart, I'm a pessimist."

Back in the control room, I noticed that the engineer, a visitor to the studio, and my call-screener all chuckled at that remark, as did the producer, who was in the studio with me. They thought it was a bit funny, and so did I. And so did Carl of Oyster Bay. Little did I realize that on that fateful day, at that critical moment, I had committed professional hara-kiri.

That comment was picked up by scores of people, recycled and amplified. A very self-righteous, pompous individual by the name of Dewayne Wickham, a journalist for *USA Today,* wrote two columns denouncing what I had said. When I saw Dewayne Wickham's vicious article against me, I began to get a little uneasy about the implications of my sarcastic comment. But I never could have imagined, it never even occurred to me, that on that day, April 16, I had done my last studio broadcast for WABC.

That fateful broadcast originated live from the famed Reo Diner in Woodbridge, New Jersey. The next day, I had a book signing for *Let's Be Heard* at Walden Books at 59 Broadway, down in the Wall Street area of New York. The signing took place from eleven thirty to one o'clock, during which I signed a few hundred books. Everybody there was very encouraging and had great things to say about my book, which made me feel very content and at ease.

Yet, lo and behold, when I got to the studio, I saw Phil Boyce on the 17th floor. Phil Boyce is the program director of WABC, having succeeded the great John Mainelli. When I saw Phil scurrying around the floor, I said to myself "oh, oh. He's not supposed to be here. He's supposed to be down in Long Boat Key." That's where the Disney people, who had just taken over ABC, were meeting with the WABC personnel.

My Piscean intuition told me that something was very, very wrong. Phil saw me as I was entering the studio, and he came up to me with a grave look on his face. "Come into my office. I have to talk to you," he said. He had never addressed me in such a curt, direct way.

We went into his office, and as he closed the door behind him, I could see that he was visibly choked up, obviously greatly disturbed. I sat down, then he sat down, not behind his desk but in a chair alongside the couch where I was sitting. He started several times to try to tell me something. I recall his stammering, "I . . . I just don't know how to tell you this, Bob."

I looked straight at him and said, "Phil, are you trying to tell me that I'm fired?"

And he looked down at the ground and replied, "Yeah . . . yeah, I am."

"But why?" I asked, dumbfounded.

And he just simply said, "the Ron Brown comment."

"The Ron Brown comment?" I couldn't believe that this was happening. I continued, "Phil, let me tell you something. It wasn't just the Ron Brown comment. They're just using that as an excuse." And indeed, ladies and gentlemen, I tell you again that they were just using that as an excuse. For, as you will see, the long knives were out to get me long before that.

I am going to reveal for the first time that there is a certain person who lives in the tri-state area—it doesn't make any difference where he lives or what his name is; that isn't important—who has been recording my program for years. This spiteful man, for some reason, has a deep and abiding hatred for me, and has also for years sworn to get me off the air. This man has been sending tapes to anybody and everybody who will listen to his case. He has been sending tapes to FAIR, a most *un*fair organization, which is a left-wing group that also has a vendetta against me. At any rate, FAIR had responded by writing an open letter to Michael Eisner, which appeared in the *NY Times* on Sunday, March 18. In that letter, they called for my removal from the airwaves for remarks that I had made, taken completely out of context, of course, in some cases back in 1991, 1992, perhaps even 1993. But certainly none of those remarks had been made by me recently.

But in the end, that didn't seem to matter. The fact is that with FAIR, with this fellow sending tapes all over the place, with vicious columns attacking me by Jack Newfield, another left-winger who has had a vendetta against me, with editorials against me in *USA Today,* management decided they didn't want any part of Bob Grant, even though I was the top ratings winner who helped make WABC the king of the hill. So, that was that. And on April 17, I was fired.

In the aftermath of that firing, all I heard were comments made by people who had attacked me. But soon after, I had a very uplifting experience as more and more people rallied to my defense. I had no idea how many fans I truly had. Not just fans, but supporters, people who loved me, and who cared very much about me and also about themselves. Because these were the people who, after I was removed from the airwaves, felt they had no voice.

At the various book signings I continued for *Let's Be Heard,* whether they were in Paramus, NJ, or Middletown, NJ, or Levittown, NY, or Stamford, CT, or wherever, people not only emotionally and sincerely asked for my autograph for their copy of the book, but often they would embrace me, sometimes almost crushing my hand with the intensity of their feeling.

Much more could be said about my firing and the fact that I am now here at WOR, especially about the role that a slime-ball by the name of Alan Dershowitz played. It is, in and of itself, an interesting story.

On the night of March 18, toward the end of his syndicated show being aired on WABC, Dershowitz took a call from a self-professed prankster by the name of Scott Pelligrino. Pelligrino asked him, "What do you think of Bob Grant?"

Now, Dershowitz hadn't mentioned me at all, but upon hearing my name, Dershowitz launched into a vicious tirade. He replied, "I think he is a racist, I think he is a bigot, and he is also a despicable talk show host."

What the public didn't know was that Dershowitz had a private grievance against me because back in October, I had decided I was sick and tired of letting him on the air anytime he chose to call the program. On that particular day in October, I had also decided not to let Dershowitz's mother, Claire, a very lovely lady who lives in Brooklyn, on the program when she called in. And why did they both want to come on my show? They wanted to team up and castigate me for slamming Dershowitz, who had earlier called police in America "professional liars," or words much to that effect.

At any rate, when Phil Boyce heard what Dershowitz had said about me in response to Pelligrino's question, Phil Boyce decided to drop Dershowitz's show immediately. When I came in the next day on the 19th of March, I asked him, "Phil, why did you drop Dershowitz?"

He said, "I don't want him saying that about another WABC talk-show host."

I thought that it was a mistake to drop the Dershowitz show for simply that reason, and apparently so did Mario Cuomo, who called me privately in my office. I hadn't spoken to Cuomo since October 30, 1986! But Cuomo importuned me to try and persuade Phil Boyce to change his mind. You see, Cuomo was under the impression that *I* had told Phil Boyce to drop the Dershowitz show. I don't think Cuomo believed me when I told him I had nothing to do with it.

Maybe Cuomo assumed people regarded the truth in the same manner he obviously does.

Anyway, after my remarks about Brown, with Dershowitz, with Newfield, with FAIR, with Wickham, with Gary Wills, with a whole host of editorial writers—with the exception of the magnificent *New York Post*—all railing against me, all piling on top of Bob Grant, how could I possibly have survived?

Well, you might say I didn't survive. Or you might say I was reborn. But the fact is that here I am at WOR, and not only on WOR but on a network, which is something I have wanted for many, many years, and with an 800 number of my own, and as they say, everything is now "peachy keen."

# I Go to Reo

◆

Let me tell you about the Reo Diner and how it came to be such an important landmark on the Bob Grant map of the world.

In 1980 I moved to Woodbridge, New Jersey, and almost every day on the way to work I would drive by a diner located on the corner of Amboy Avenue, near Main Street. For almost five years I drove by, barely noticing it, because I was not—*am* not—a diner person.

And then one day, in June of 1985, I got a letter from a woman who enclosed a photo from her neighborhood newspaper. Her letter said, "Here are some of the immigrants that you talk about, the type of Americans you laud on the show. Thought you would like to know about these fine people, since I go to the Reo Diner all the time."

And the photo showed the owners of the Reo Diner, Mike Forakis, a native-born American of Greek descent, who served in the United States Marines in World War II, together with his partner and brother-in-law, Teddy Likakis, who was born in Greece and came to America when he was fifteen years old, in 1950. And they were raising the American flag. It was Flag Day, and the caption said that every day is Flag Day at the Reo Diner, because they raise the American flag every day. The paper also quoted Teddy as saying that when

232

he came to this country, he had no shoes, but now he is a very comfortable man, doing very well. He said, "Only in America." That was his phrase, said just as so many others have said it. "Only in America." And because of that, and because his brother-in-law Mike fought in the Pacific, I praised them on the air. I paid tribute to them. Although I had yet to set foot inside their establishment.

A short while later, I head from this lady again. She said they would love it if I could send an autographed photo, because they have pictures of celebrities hanging on the wall behind the cash register, and they would like to put my picture up. *Well,* I thought, *what the hell—why* send *it? I pass the Reo practically every day. I'm going to just drop in.*

So I autographed the photo—"To my friends at the Reo"—and I put it in an envelope, and I brought it to the diner. I was so *proud* of the fact that here I was, the great and humble Bob Grant, making a personal appearance to deliver my signed celebrity portrait. I said to the fellow behind the counter, "Is Teddy Likakis here?" And the guy said, "No, not here." So I said, "Oh. Well, I heard that he wanted a photo of me, and I thought I'd bring it over." And the guy says, "Oh, yeah? Okay, I'll give it to him." I then said, "I'm Bob Grant." To which he replied, "Oh. Hi." I was talking to Teddy's partner, Mike Forakis, I later learned, and Mike did *not* listen to my show. Teddy did—in fact, Teddy was a big fan—but back then Mike listened to music. Hence, he was underwhelmed, you might say, by my appearance, not to mention my picture.

Well, when Teddy came in the next day, he was mortified. *What?? Bob Grant was here?? OH, MIKE—YOU DON'T REALIZE WHAT YOU DID!!* And so forth and so on.

Teddy had the letter-writing woman call me, and she said, "Oh, please, Mr. Grant, stop in again." And I did, and it became a hangout of mine, and since then we have become friends—real friends. They're like family to me, wonderful people. I even do radio programs from there. As a matter of fact, every year the whole station participates in a leukemia fund-raising event broadcast from the Reo Diner. We raise a lot of money—maybe $30,000 in a three-hour period.

The Reo has become my New Jersey office and home away

from home, to the point where I now receive a lot of unsolicited mail there. When I lived close by, I used to stop in many times a week. Now I visit maybe once a week or so, but it continues to hold a special place in my heart. I wish I could get there more often, because, quite frankly, they make me feel very comfortable. I have my own table there, and they tell me that people come in and ask, "Where does Bob Grant sit when he's here?" And they say, "Right there." I've been told by waitresses that people actually go over and touch the chair. Or they'll ask, "What does he eat?" One time I was there, having my breakfast, and I heard a woman exclaim, *"Ooh,* he's eating a corn muffin!"

Sadly, by the time this book comes out, Mike will be dead. They just sent him home from New York Hospital because there's nothing more that doctors can do for him. He had prostate cancer that spread to his bones and everywhere else. Very, very sad. The doctors told his family, "Either take him home or send him to a hospice." And, being Greek and very traditional, they're *not* going to send him to a hospice.

Since I put the Reo Diner on the map, every politician in New Jersey goes there to campaign. Even Flim-Flam Florio went there. I know this because I went to the Reo one day and saw Florio signs all over, and I promptly ripped them down. Even Senator Lousenberg has paid his respects to the Reo Diner—not when *I* was there, of course.

# Ten Things We Can Do to Keep America Great

———— ◆ ————

1. *Teach everybody American history.* And I mean *real* history, not let's-pretend history, not make-everybody-feel-good history, not multicultural history, not crybaby history, not the history of divisiveness. The history of the *United* States, of *e pluribus unum.* America has worked as a home to people from every continent only because of its wise, humane western European ideals. *That's* what everybody in this country needs to understand and remember, and what is history's purpose if not to teach the truths that must not be forgotten?

2. *Create real borders.* Because by definition, a country without boundaries is not a country. It's just a land mass ripe for the picking by any scavenger who shows up. And by real borders I mean inviolable lines.

3. *Enact the Bob Grant Mandatory Sterilization Program.* We have far too many children being born to parents who are either nowhere to be found or completely unable to provide a stable, loving, nurturing, *self-sustaining* home. And I'm tired of hearing how welfare doesn't really cost the taxpayers all that much—because the toll is taken in more than dollars and cents. We're providing prenatal and natal and postnatal care and supporting the family today, and then tomorrow, once those kiddies grow up to be teenage sociopaths, we're human prey to marauding wolfpacks. (Until, of course, we

have to support them in prison.) If you can't pay your own way, then you *certainly* can't afford to have a child, it's simple as that. So women of childbearing years who want welfare must agree to undergo temporary sterilization via Norplant or some other safe chemical method. Once they're off the dole, they can multiply like bunnies—as long as they can afford it. Just like everybody else.

4. *Get serious with the death penalty.* Once violent career criminals have declared war on us, let's respond appropriately. Don't lock them up, because they're never going to "reform," no matter how long they're in jail. These thugs behave like they're at war with us; let's take the same attitude about the "sanctity" of their lives as we do about those of our foreign enemies in time of war.

5. *Renew our faith in free speech.* Not just in the letter of the First Amendment, but in the spirit of the principle behind it: that people can be trusted to weigh all sides of an argument and then do what they believe is right. I agree with Voltaire, who called freedom of opinion "the life of the soul." No more speech codes on campus, on newspaper op-ed pages, or anywhere else in American life. They're un-American.

6. *Renew our vows as Americans.* Let's remind ourselves that we must act as one people, not many, if we're going to prosper. Over the past three decades we've had enough coddling of special interests and splinter groups to last a lifetime. From here on, the first question is this: Does the action under consideration benefit the nation as a whole? If it does, fine. But if it helps one small segment at the expense of the rest of us, it's by definition a bad, divisive thing, and should be defeated. No more reparations or make-goods. Let's act like we're all in the same boat for a while and see what happens.

7. *Insist on better entertainment.* Everybody complains about violence on TV, vulgarity on radio, pornography at the movies, so who's making all those studios and networks rich? The entertainment media have a vast influence over our lives. They fill every moment of silence we used to enjoy. We can improve what we get by no longer watching or listening to anything that offends us. It doesn't require any big, organized

boycott. Just stop. Don't worry about whether the garbage ceases or not. You'll have gotten it out of your life. The executives will notice soon enough.

8. *Insist on common sense in government.* I usually hate any kind of political "litmus test," but here's one I'll endorse. From now on, let's examine every proposal before Congress and all state and local legislative bodies to see just one thing: Does it make sense? Does the principle behind this action sound logical and rational and practical? Does it sound like something you'd try in your own life? If it's just more pie-in-the-sky, more appeasement of special interests, more pandering for votes regardless of what the law really *does,* our representatives must vote against it. You don't have to be a law professor to know whether a law will be good or bad for us, regardless of what anybody tells you.

9. *Vote Republican across the board this year.* It's not as though I'm in love with the Republican party, but they're on a roll to bring sanity back to government. They need as big a majority in both houses as possible. Our national turnout on election days is disgraceful. This year, vote.

10. *Read this book.* Read it in public, where others can see it. Read it to your children at bedtime. Read it to your liberal sister-in-law. Read it in the tub. Read it to the blind. I had a lot of fun writing it, and I'd hate to keep all that enjoyment to myself. America deserves this book.

"Oh, I've read it," she said.

"Then you didn't read page thirteen very closely," I said.

We turned to the page, whereupon she read the author's description of yours truly. He wrote that I am "the king of talk radio in New York. . . . He is one of the few talk show hosts who has lasted in combat radio. He defined it and spawned countless imitators all over the country. Nobody does it better than he does and his ratings are proof. If New York is an argument, and it is, then Bob Grant's show is New York every day."

And—*dammit!*—the woman instantly began to look upon me with a whole new respect and admiration. Even worse: I had revealed my shameful secret, that I'd actually *memorized* the number of the page on which the author lavished me with praise.

Is there any higher compliment I can pay him?

Oh, wait, maybe this: When I surf through TV channels with my remote control, I must be ever vigilant just in case I accidently come upon a station that's carrying his show. Because the mere sight of him, and the knowledge that countless millions of Americans are absolutely riveted to the screen when his presence graces it, can send me into a funk. I also have to be on guard walking through malls and airports, lest I spy a store window displaying his books or magazines whose covers feature his image. I've given up trying to get through a newspaper without tripping over his name a dozen or so times.

There—is it possible to heap my praise any higher?

To explain all this angst, let's flash back for a moment to a time twenty or so years ago. I was doing pretty much the same show I do now—abrasive and hateful to some, gratifying and highly entertaining to others, but unmistakably, inarguably, guaranteed-one-hundred-percent *conservative.* Back when we were still scuffling over issues like forced busing and the Soviet plan for world domination, I was the *only* broadcaster in town (or anywhere else, for that matter) who espoused the rock-ribbed conservative point of view and got good ratings doing it.

It might seem like it was a lonely life, but to be honest, I loved being out there on my own. Every other media figure

was mouthing the idiotic liberal line (this was New York in its lefty Democratic heyday, remember). And I was different. Special. Maybe even unique. I had a true-blue following of listeners who used to say, "Bob, if we didn't have you, we wouldn't have *anything.*" This stuff made it all worthwhile.

And things remained that way until some time during Ronald Reagan's terms in the White House. That's when conservatism began to take on a certain glamour, an undeniable vigor. We were no longer being misrepresented as a bunch of gun nuts, Birchers, antifluoridation freaks, apocalypse junkies, closet Klansmen, and crazed paranoiacs. It's clear, looking back, that the conservative point of view lacked but one thing—a leading man.

It was only a matter of time, of course. That's why, even now, I need refer to him only as The Great Inevitable One for you to know whom I mean.

I still remember my first eyeful of the flier announcing his arrival here from a station in Sacramento. Well, well, I thought, some young conservative buck is trying to start up a network talk-radio show. The satellite technology, finally, was in place to allow such a thing. Good luck to him.

Then he himself arrived in town. Among his first stops was a visit to me. He was a true gentleman. I remember his words: "Your reputation precedes you, sir," he said.

Did what followed all happen overnight? It seems that way to me now. But how?

Well, first of all, the satellite made him the first *national* media figure who dared to refuse to spout the liberal party line. Every American who had grown sick of the knee-jerk lefties who run broadcasting raised a cheer when they heard him speak. And people like tuning in to someone who's being heard all across the country. It gives listeners the sense that they're part of something truly *big.*

Second, and most important, he did his show with a sense of humor. It signaled how low the liberal philosophy had fallen when, instead of railing and raging against it, people began to *laugh* at it. For years, liberals had mocked conservatives. Now, finally, the shoe was on the other foot, and it fit just fine. He confounded the stereotype of how a conservative sounded: he was downright amiable and amused. His deliv-

ery, his voice—all easy on the ears. He likes to call himself "just a lovable fuzzball," and he really is, professionally and personally.

But did he *have* to attract twenty million fanatic followers? Did he *have* to inspire such devotion, such loyalty, that his fans would snap up books, coffee mugs, T-shirts, and anything else with his handsome visage on it? Did he *have* to become practically synonymous with the revitalized brand of conservatism that's getting this country back on the right track? Did he *have* to turn into a national obsession?

Even worse, because broadcasting is essentially a followers' medium, his success has inspired the proliferation of more public conservatives on TV, radio, and in print than I can count. Now people say to me, "We wouldn't have anybody on our side, Bob, if it weren't for you . . . and that guy and that guy and that guy and that guy . . ."

Of course, I am a big enough person to acknowledge that while he may have made my life a little less special, he has done more for the conservative cause than anybody realizes. In fact, I truly believe that if he wants to put all his influence to good use, he would take a leading role in the elections this year. Maybe even run for something. Maybe even president. I have no doubt he'd win. But that job would leave him no time at all for a radio show.

Rush in ninety-six!

# *The Most Disgusting*
# *Sound on Radio Today*

——— ◆ ———

THERE'S LIVING PROOF THAT THE MOST IMPORTANT FACTOR IN THE life of a successful person is the timing of his birth, and its name is Howard Stern.

If he had come into radio twenty years earlier, his brand of "humor" would have earned him a fast ticket home. Twenty years from now, the airwaves will be so degraded that nothing will shock us. This is not a reflection on him—he didn't decide when to be born—but on what he has to offer to American listeners today.

If you've never had the pleasure of hearing his show, I can describe its singular defining characteristic: He's famous for turning unpleasant natural functions into his own signature sounds. He fetishizes what the rest of us would never even mention *off* the air. He's like a baby digging around delightedly in his own diaper.

That he has become rich and famous for doing that tells me how low we have sunk. He's probably the most popular figure in radio today, so what does that say about us? Nothing good, I assure you.

He prides himself on his fearlessness, but he displayed his true nature when the Latino singer Selena was murdered. He actually found something to laugh about in that tragedy. Then, when her fans protested, he whined that he was only

making fun of Latino music, not of her death. Which is a lie, pure and simple: During his "commentary" on what happened, he played Mexican music overdubbed with the sound of gunshots. He's a hypocrite and a coward.

So, I find him disgusting, but I have to admit there have been times he's made me laugh. He's actually capable of intelligent, biting mockery of political correctness and hypersensitivity about race and ethnicity. But that's not why he's famous. His success is due mainly to his favorite four-letter word, which starts with an F and ends with a T and reminds me of nothing so much as the sound of Howard Stern's voice.

# *Academia Nuts*

———— ◆ ————

THERE'S BUT ONE PLACE LEFT ON THE FACE OF THE EARTH WHERE widespread belief in the goodness and rightness of the principles of communism still endures. It's not in Russia or anywhere else in what was the Soviet Union. It's not in Cuba, that's for certain, or in Angola or Mozambique or Prague or Warsaw or Vietnam, either. You'll guess incorrectly all day if I let you, so I'll end the mystery now:

It's in American universities.

It's been said, only half-facetiously, that there are more communists on the campuses of America than there ever were in Red Square.

Now, I'm not talking about card-carrying members of the Communist Party USA or KGB spies or anything like what went on in academia when it still looked like the reds had a shot at ruling the world. I'm talking about philosophical communists. All-talk communists. Lip-service commies of the heart, mind, and soul.

The cruelly enforced egalitarianism and anti-elitism of Stalin and Mao are still going strong on campus. So are the virulent anti-Americanism and anticapitalism. And the refusal to allow dissent or free and open exchanges of opinion hearkens back to the days when the threat of the gulag kept millions under mental lock and key. The thought-thugs who

staff America's colleges like to think of themselves as the party rulers, and the students as the proletariat.

It's almost hilarious—until you remember that those students are our future, and we're paying the tab for these academic exercises in tyranny and nihilism.

I remember when I took my freshman social studies course, the inevitable 101. The teacher was a woman, Miss Franklin, and even though I was an innocent babe, I looked at her on the first day of class and said to myself, "This ugly broad is a pinko red commie." And in fact, whenever she would say "Soviet Union" or "Joseph Stalin" or "the New Deal," she would smile.

Then, lo and behold, years later I was reading a book that named members of the Communist Party USA, and whose name did I find? I thought, how many other Miss Franklins must there be out there teaching young people? Maybe they weren't all staunch party members, but what were they teaching? Which value system were they praising? What were they doing to rewrite history?

These were the same American intellectuals who couldn't bring themselves to condemn Stalin even after communist totalitarianism had been unmasked in the eyes of the rest of the world. Faithful reds in eastern Europe, Italy, France, Spain, and elsewhere turned their backs on the cause after the 1968 Czechoslovakian Spring, when Russian troops crushed freedom in that gentle country. In the U.S., though, nothing changed. Lillian Hellman never denounced Stalin, and she was but one of many highbrows who refused to see communism for what it truly was.

I have come to the conclusion that the American communists believed in their cause not because they hoped it would improve their country, but because they hoped it would destroy it. They weren't really *for* socialism. They were just *against* democracy and capitalism and freedom. Our communists, unlike those elsewhere, just hated *any* system that worked. Like most Americans, our commies were apolitical. They were espresso anarchists—misfits, malcontents, and neurotics.

The current crop of professors—the deconstructionists, the postconstructionists, the New History and New Criticism crowd—are the intellectual heirs to those losers. Academia is now a dangerous place for a youngster to go, because he or she

can pick up some nasty misinformation. College kids call me on the air all the time now. Now so long ago, a young person wouldn't be caught dead calling a show like mine. That they do is evidence of the kind of mistreatment they're getting at school.

They'll call and tell me how they're being taught, for instance, that the United States was responsible for the Cold War. How, as communism fell, the United States was trying to undermine stability in the Soviet Union. Just the opposite of what really went on.

Or they'll report that they're made to feel that they live in occupied territory or that Christopher Columbus was one of history's worst war criminals. Young white males in particular say they're treated as though they've done something horribly wrong, that they're responsible for current as well as historical oppression of blacks and Latinos and women and homosexuals.

Today, courses in history, political science, literature, sociology, and other disciplines are being taught by "ethnic studies" instructors. Can anybody explain the logic in that? Or in something called "gay and lesbian studies"? Since when is history either gay *or* straight? Since when is literature black, brown, yellow, *or* white? If "sociology" is not a woman, why is it being taught under the heading of "women's studies"? At this rate, we'll never again have a course simply titled American History. We'll have courses in white female history, white male history (maybe), black female history, black male history, gay white female history, gay black female history, disabled gay white female history, fragrance-sensitive disabled gay black female history, and so on. Any day now, I swear, high school kids will be required to study bisexual algebra.

These are not studies. This is not scholarship. It's a flimsy grab bag of courses that should be titled "Feel-Good-About-Yourself 101," "Advanced Let's-Pander-to-Minorities-So-They-Won't-Occupy-the-Dean's-Office," and "Introduction to Give-Unqualified-Students-the-False-Sense-That-They're-Getting-an-Education." It's no coincidence that the rise of ethnic and gender studies was accompanied by the advent of speech codes on campus, those loathsome rules that prohibit freedom of expression in order to keep somebody's tender feelings from getting bruised.

When I went to school, we were encouraged to believe that our ethnicity, race, gender, or religion were all immaterial. We were taught that who we were inside was all that would count as we made our way through life. Today, students are being taught just the opposite—that who they are as individuals is meaningless and that only differences in race and background determine who we *really* are. How will that help resolve the divisiveness currently afflicting our country? It won't. In fact, it will make things far worse in the future.

Another difference from when I went to school is that back then, we had to *learn*. We had to take real courses, in science and mathematics and the humanities, where we were expected to absorb information and ideas. Sounds quaint, doesn't it? All the current academic concentration on grievances has effectively moved the focus off of *learning*. College today isn't about learning, you see. It's there to help our campus commies to advance beliefs that the rest of the thinking world has been laughing at for more than four decades.

# American Psychobabble

———— ◆ ————

A FAIR NUMBER OF AMERICANS ARE RICH ENOUGH TO BE BEYOND having to worry about survival and solvency. A smaller set within that group are also widely adored, worshipped, admired figures who receive more than their fair share of attention. That crowd—actors, artists, certain tycoons, some politicians and media types, the A-list—would seem to have it all. They have managed to fulfill the two most basic human hungers, for sustenance and love.

There's something else they have in common: they all seem to need psychiatrists.

Honestly, when was the last time you read about one of these fortunate figures without reading about their dependence upon some analyst or therapist of one sort or another? Some see their shrink five days a week. Some continue going for years and years. "My shrink, my shrink, my shrink . . ." they blather on.

Here's my question—what exactly do these individuals need to have *shrunk*?

A cynic might say their salaries and egos are what require a little downsizing. If they had to live like mere mortals and worry about things like tuition bills and promotions at the office and mortgage and car and insurance payments, maybe they'd have less time and energy for such self-absorption.